The Restaurant Start-Up Guide

Peter Rainsford
and
David H. Bangs, Jr.

Upstart
Publishing Company
Specializing in Small Business Publishing
a division of Dearborn Publishing Group, Inc.

Executive Editor: Cynthia A. Zigmund
Managing Editor: Jack Kiburz
Interior Design: Eliot House Productions
Cover Design: Vince DePinto, DePinto Studios

Published by Upstart Publishing Company,
a division of Dearborn Publishing Group, Inc.

Printed in the United States of America

97 98 99 10 9 8 7 6 5 4 3 2 1

Library of Congress Cataloging-in-Publication Data
Rainsford, Peter.
    The restaurant start-up guide / Peter Rainsford, David H. Bangs, Jr.
        p.   cm.
    Includes index.
    ISBN 1-57410-071-8 (pbk.)
    1. Restaurant management. 2. New business enterprises—Planning.
    I. Bangs, David H. II. Title.
    TX911.3.M27R36 1997   97-13871
    647.95'068—dc21   CIP

Upstart books are available at special quality discounts to use as premiums and sales promotions, or for use in corporate training programs. For more information, please call the Special Sales Manager at 800-621-9621, ext. 4384, or write to Dearborn Financial Publishing, Inc., 155 N. Wacker Drive, Chicago, IL 60606-1719.

Table of Contents

Introduction

SO YOU WANT TO START A RESTAURANT! You are not alone. Thousands of other people have the same dream, and many actually start restaurants. Others never get that far.

It's New Year's Eve, 1996, and I'm sitting in a beautiful log home owned by Jan and Bill Van Straaten in Clark, Colorado which is about 25 miles north of Steamboat Springs in the middle of the Routt National Forest. There's a fire in the fireplace, it's snowing outside, and Bill is cooking something that smells wonderful. The idea for this book originated here.

Jan and Bill are wonderful friends who have been kind enough to invite my family and me to spend New Year's with them for the past four years. Bill loves to cook, and when he designed their log home he decided to put in a commercial kitchen. Bill and I do the cooking—and try to stay out of each other's way—and the rest of our families do the eating. (We won't discuss the clean up aspects!) In any case, several years ago Jan and Bill were thinking about opening a restaurant and much of our conversation during that holiday was devoted to discussing how to do so. Jan and Bill asked lots of questions. I answered some of their questions. I stared blankly at others. As a result of that discussion, I realized that other hopeful restaurateurs probably had similar questions—and the idea for this book was developed.

With annual sales exceeding $300 billion, the food service industry is the largest retail industry in the United States. The industry employs over nine million people in more than 750,000 food service establishments and, on a typical day, almost one-half of all adults are food service patrons.

The typical restaurant is really a small business. Consider the following statistics from the National Restaurant Association:

- More than nine out of 10 restaurants had fewer than 50 paid employees in 1992.

- More than two out of three restaurants had annual sales of less than $500,000 in 1992.

- Forty-five percent of all restaurants are either sole proprietorships or partnerships.

- Three out of four restaurants are single-unit operations.

- Forty-two percent of adult females and 31 percent of adult males have worked in the food service industry at some point in their life.

Successful restaurateurs need all the skills and knowledge that other small business owners need to succeed. This book is designed to help you evaluate whether or not your restaurant idea makes sense, to increase your chances of success, and to reduce the chances of failure.

It is difficult to say how many business start-ups—let alone restaurants—actually survive. A number of studies reveal a wide variety of statistics and most deal with small businesses in general. To get a better understanding of restaurant failure rates (or, more properly, restaurant success rates), I asked one of my colleagues here at the Cornell University School of Hotel Administration, Professor Chris Muller, since he has done extensive research on the subject. Professor Muller's research has shown that about one-third of all restaurants will fail in the first year of operation. Of those remaining, another one-third will fail in the second year of operation. For those still in operation in year three, the chances of success become much better—65 percent will make it to 10 years. Therefore, the third year is critical. If you can make it that far, your chances of success are greatly enhanced. Professor Muller suggests that, if you are thinking of buying or selling a restaurant, do so in its third year of operation. These figures are reflective of all restaurants. For franchised restaurants, only 10 percent fail in the first year and 85 percent are still operating under the same ownership after five years. This book doesn't specifically examine franchises—although many of the principles and suggestions certainly apply—but they are an important part of the industry and may be something you want to explore.

This book is directed to another segment of restaurateurs—those of you who are planning on succeeding in the restaurant business. Our credentials as authors come from over 60 years of combined small business experience and surviving most of the mistakes newcomers to small business ownership tend to make. In 1977, David H. Bangs, Jr. started his own small business, Upstart Publishing Company, Inc. It was a fairly typical start up: undercapitalized; uncertain about markets, products, and pricing; and touch and go for the first few years. His only regret was not having embarked on his enterprise sooner. In addition to my responsibilities as a faculty member at Cornell University's School of Hotel Administration—where I have taught a variety of courses in food and beverage management and where I am now teaching one course in strategic management and another in entrepreneurship and small business management—I have owned and operated a variety of small businesses (including five years as a restaurateur). Some have been successful. Others have not. And my failures are probably more valuable to you than my successes.

In addition to our own experiences, we thought it might be helpful to provide you with a broader perspective about the trials and tribulations of starting your own restaurant. In order to do so, we designed and sent a survey to successful restaurateurs—success being defined by the fact that they were still in business. Eighty-nine restaurateurs responded and took the time to answer the 67 questions we asked. The typical respondent has been in business for almost 15 years and operates a full-service restaurant which has an average check of between $10.00 and $14.99 and has annual sales of between $501,000 and $1,000,000. Almost all are independent rather than franchised restaurants. We are extremely grateful for the comments and information that these restaurateurs provided—and even more grateful that they took the time out of their busy schedules to complete the questionnaire. Throughout this book we will share their valuable thoughts, ideas, and comments with you.

Most small businesses will succeed, provided their owners are determined, stubborn, and willing to take control of those variables that can be controlled. Changes in markets, competition, products, and customer perceptions are inevitable. Restaurants that can adapt to such changes because of their owner's foresight and careful planning will profit. Those that become rigid won't make it.

A restaurant owner who fails to plan plans to fail. We believe this cliché and have noticed time and time again that small business owners who take the time to think through their strategies, use information to balance their enthusiasm, and are smart enough to recognize their own limitations don't fail. A formal written business plan is a great tool for controlling a business and maintaining focus—but we've also seen very successful restaurants where the owner keeps the plan in his or her head. Because none of us is immortal, however, this risk is unnecessary. Restaurateurs face plenty of risks as it is without adding to the list. A written business plan is helpful in so many ways that the time and effort to write and update it are trifling in comparison to the benefits it gives. This book is not designed to show you how to write a business plan, although much of the information will have to be included in a business plan. For a detailed guide to writing a business plan for a restaurant, we strongly recommend *The Restaurant*

Planning Guide. It's extremely well written and extremely useful. (It's also written by us!)

Since the process of starting a restaurant is long and complex, be aware of the benefits of allowing yourself the full amount of time that this book suggests (or longer). Spending six months to a year before making one of the biggest investments you'll ever make (both financially and personally) gives you time to modify your initial ideas, acquire the skills and information that will set your restaurant apart from the ordinary, and ensure your success. Potentially disastrous management errors such as undercapitalization, negative cash flow, poor hiring choices, and choosing the wrong location can and should be avoided. For example, in a Small Business Administration survey the most common answer to the question "Why did you choose this location?" was "noticed vacancy." Don't make the same mistake unless you want your restaurant to fail.

To help you organize both your thoughts and your time, we have included extensive checklists to get you started. The chapters in the book are organized according to time periods—measured in the number of months before you open for business. At the end of each chapter is a detailed action plan which reminds you of the items that need to be accomplished and provides space for you to plan your tactics and check-off the item once it has been completed. We have also included a detailed restaurant facilities and operations review as Appendix A. It contains over 700 items that you should be concerned with once your restaurant opens. It should also be extremely valuable to you before opening to identify those things—both physical facilities and operational issues—that you must plan for.

Take your time. If you can, work for someone else—or better yet, several different people—for a while to learn the ins and outs of the restaurant business. Take courses to improve your general management and restaurant management skills. Keep a notebook with ideas about your restaurant's benefits, the markets you plan to serve, the competition, and any other scrap of information that might give you a competitive edge. Jot down ideas about how to serve your new boss (that is, your customers and guests) better than anyone else. What kind of prices will you charge? What level of service makes sense for your restaurant? Etc., etc., etc.

Most important of all, make sure that meeting the demands of business ownership is consistent with your other goals in life. Small businesses can make you rich, but that might not be worth the dedication such a goal calls for. You have to balance your business and personal goals, or you won't attain either. By now you should have noticed that we refer to restaurants as well as "your business" or "small businesses." It's intentional. Restaurants are businesses, and as such you will need a whole variety of skills and talents to succeed. If you like to cook and, therefore, think that's all you need to know to open a restaurant, stop now! You won't succeed!

Good luck with your restaurant. I hope you'll find owning your own restaurant as exciting and rewarding as I have.

—Peter Rainsford
Clark, Colorado
December 31, 1996

(P.S., In case you're wondering, Jan and Bill Van Straaten decided not to open a restaurant in Steamboat Springs, Colorado. They did, however, start several other successful entrepreneurial ventures including Ceramica, a delightful store in Steamboat Springs that sells the most wonderful hand painted Italian pottery. Give Jan or Bill a call at 800-467-8989 and get a catalog!)

ONE

The Basics of Business Ownership

YOU CAN DO IT. YOU CAN BE ONE OF THE THOUSANDS of people who will start a successful restaurant during the next 12 months. This book will help you establish and follow a process which will culminate in establishing the right restaurant for you, based on your abilities, interests, goals, and resources.

It will take hard work. The most this *Guide* can do is to show you directions, pose questions, and suggest ways to arrive at the answers. You have to provide the detailed answers and, in the process, will learn a lot about whether or not you should be in business for yourself.

This is particularly important for those of you who have suddenly found yourself unemployed due to downsizing, outsourcing, corporate re-engineering, or any of the other euphemisms for unanticipated early retirement. The lure of self-employment is strong—but the very qualities which made you successful in a larger business or organization may work against you. For example, the ability to follow instructions flawlessly is useless if you have no instructions. High technical abilities in a limited area, such as corporate finance, are not readily transferred to a small business, where more general skills are needed. Few people in a Fortune 1,000 company get to see the entire "big picture" including the competitive, economic, political, environmental, social, and strategic environments the restaurant operates in. As discussed in the introduction, most restaurants are small businesses and in a small business you have to do it all: finance, operations, marketing, personnel, sales, public relations and on and on. You won't have corporate services to rely on. It isn't that you cannot transfer many skills and much experience. The small business experience is just so very different from the corporate experience that a lot of un-learning has to take place before you can move forward.

As an example, Andy once started a business with a high-level banker, a highly intelligent and skilled man with a DBA and years of experience. The small business world was utterly foreign to him, full of uncertainties (such as an irregular paycheck!) and duties that he hadn't had to perform before: running the copier, sweeping the floor, calling slow-paying accounts, and hardest of all, selling a product to a reluctant market. He missed the benefits, status, and power of his banking job. He missed the socializing too, the long lunches with other executives, the meetings with interesting and powerful clients. He lasted less than a year before scurrying back to a comfortable institutional position. In that world he was and is very effective. He wasn't able to make the transition to the alien and uncertain world of small business. This is no reflection on him; it is simply the way small business affected him. We couldn't last a month in his world. He at least lasted ten months in ours.

The conflict between the structures and practices of big vs. small businesses can be overcome, of course. Many people have made the jump successfully. But it takes time. As more and more people in the entrepreneurial '90s make the shift from working in big organizations to starting and running their own businesses, those of you who make haste slowly will come out ahead. Take your time. Habits and expectations that took years to develop don't go away overnight.

Chapters Two through Eight contain Action Plans to help you organize your time and use it effectively and purposefully. Some of the suggested actions can only be done by you; others should be done with the help of others; some can only be performed by experts, those professionals whom experienced business owners make sure to have on their team. The suggested actions should be taken in sequence, but you may have special talents or experiences which will help you shorten the cycle by combining various steps. You may choose to ignore or minimize some of the actions. That's up to you, but you do so at your own peril. For example, you may not feel you have the time or opportunity to work for someone else and gain experience in the restaurant business. Ideally, you should work for a similar kind of restaurant for a year or so in a management capacity, but you may have experience that is equivalent, or perhaps you can find courses or workshops to speed up the learning and experience the curves.

Even before starting the process, ask yourself some tough questions about your fitness for owning and operating a business. Business ownership is an important part of the American dream, but it is not right for everyone. Qualities that make a difference between success and failure include perseverance, stamina (emotional as well as physical) to put in the energy only the owner provides, courage to ride out tight times, ability to make decisions on incomplete knowledge, communication skills, and willingness to take limited (not careless) risks. Not everyone has these qualities.

You needn't be a genius to have a profitable start-up. You do need common sense, and should be willing to face and accept your own limitations.

Successful business people seek out and follow the best advice they can. Refusal to seek out and follow such advice is a good way to guarantee failure and is not evidence of strength of character. Outside advisors help you make decisions based on facts, not wishful thinking, provide a reality check, and can give you insights that help your business run better. This is particularly helpful in the pre-start-up phase, because you probably don't know what questions to ask. This book poses some questions, but each restaurant and each location will present specific questions that no book, no matter how detailed, could anticipate.

The Six Myths of Business Ownership

Business ownership is surrounded by myths. Don't fall for the following, which are common and dangerous.

1. *I can bootstrap it.* Undercapitalization (too little money invested in the business) is the biggest cause of small business failure and usually results in negative cash flow (more going out than coming in). While you may indeed be able to bootstrap a restaurant, why take the risk when you can calculate the amount of capital investment needed to make your venture succeed? This cash reserve makes you sleep better, helps avoid panicky decisions, and gives you the breathing room needed to run your business.

2. *I can start living off the restaurant immediately.* Forget it. Most restaurant owners find that it takes between six months and a year—if not longer—before their business can pay them a decent wage. Early expenses always outrun early revenues. For this reason alone, be prepared to live on savings (or have another income supporting you) until your restaurant can afford to pay you.

3. *I'll be my own boss.* Not likely. The restaurant and its customers will be your boss and keep you occupied 60 or more hours a week. Your other bosses include employees, vendors, bankers, and investors.

4. *I'll get rich overnight.* You won't. The get-rich-quick stories are either bogus (the many years of preparation are hidden) or so unusual that your chances of winning the lottery are higher. Small businesses are a great way to build wealth, but it takes time. David Birch, the eminent small business researcher, notes that more than one-third of businesses which grow significantly don't do so until they've been active for ten or more years.

5. *I have nothing to lose.* I'll incorporate and use other people's money. Hogwash. The "corporate shield" only exists in rare cases where the business is strongly capitalized and big enough to make creditors (suppliers, bankers, investors) rest easy. Start-ups seldom meet these criteria. The same applies to using OPM (Other People's Money), in spite of all the books and articles urging you to borrow your way to wealth. It isn't that

To help you understand why other people started their own restaurants, we asked the restaurateurs in our survey why they had started. The overriding reasons were clearly to work for themselves and to pursue a dream. Most were realistic about the financial rewards and didn't expect to make a fortune. In fact, one respondent stated, "Question: How do you make a small fortune? Answer: Get yourself a big fortune and go into the restaurant business!"

For each of the following items, please indicate how important it was for opening your first restaurant.

	"1"	"2"	"3"	"4"	"5"	Avg.
To work for yourself?	3.6%	7.2%	13.3%	22.9%	53.0%	4.1
To create a vision/ pursue a dream?	3.6%	6.0%	19.3%	32.5%	38.6%	4.0
To provide a secured income?	6.0%	14.5%	37.3%	25.3%	16.9%	3.3
To improve the quality of restaurants in the marketplace?	26.5%	6.0%	26.5%	25.3%	15.7%	3.0
To create a legacy??	45.1%	17.1%	19.5%	12.2%	2.2%	1.9

"1" = Not Important
"2" = Slightly Important
"3" = Important
"4" = Very Important
"5" = Extremely Important

NOTE: With all our comparative survey questions, a response of "1" was low and a response of "5" was high. Also, the average indicates the average response of all people responding to that question. The higher the average, the more important that item is. Thus, in this case, the most important reason for starting a restaurant was to work for themselves, the next most important reason was to create a vision or pursue a dream, and the least important reason was to create a legacy.

easy to find OPM—and it never makes business sense to take on debt if you can avoid it.

6. *It takes money to make money.* This one's a half-truth. Bankers are extremely reluctant to loan money for restaurant start-ups unless you have substantial collateral to support the loan. On the other hand, there are ways to lower the costs of going into the restaurant business. Leasing a building rather than purchasing or constructing is one. Buying used kitchen equipment and used dining room furniture and fixtures is another. Leasing an existing, fully equipped restaurant is a third—but carefully investigate why the restaurant went out of business before signing on the dotted line.

How to Lower the Risks of a Start-Up

The following are proven ways to lower the inherent risks of starting your own restaurant and are worth incorporating in your start-up plans:

• Get experience in management and in the type of restaurant you plan to start. Experience is not the only way to learn, but it is still the best teacher. Combine experience with course work and study and participation in trade groups, and you have an almost unbeatable start towards business success.

• Plan ahead. The action orientation many entrepreneurs pride themselves on has to be tempered with foresight and careful planning. A written business plan is inexpensive insurance. It will help you focus on the important parts of your business, use your resources wisely and consistently, and save a lot of trouble. Use our *Restaurant Planning Guide* to help you set up and write your business plan.

• Make sure you have your family's support. Even though you're not devoting 168 hours a week to your business, your family will think you are. If your family understands and is willing to provide the emotional support

you'll need during the start-up period, your chances improve dramatical-
ly. The impact of uncertain income, demands on your time and attention
that will preoccupy you 24 hours a day for months at a stretch, and the
sheer anxiety of being the responsible owner of a restaurant puts a strain
on the best relationships.

- Be prepared to become tired and discouraged and still persevere. It goes
  with the territory. Stamina is important. So is persistence, because when
  things get tough (and they will) it's very easy to give up. Experts like to
  talk about the "five-yard-line phenomenon," in which a business owner
  presses on and on against huge odds, gets discouraged, and quits or
  makes a dumb mistake when the goal line is within reach. Starting a
  restaurant from scratch is hard. You (and you alone) have to provide the
  impetus to get things going and keep them going. You don't have the
  built-in momentum that a going business has. The consistent inputting of
  energy can become draining, but you have to do it.

- Use facts to substantiate your insights and hunches before acting on them.
  Decisions based on facts are far more likely to be good decisions than
  those based on whim. Your restaurant is too important to risk on the consequences of a lot of hasty decisions. An idea that still seems sound after
  you sleep on it probably is a good idea. Remember the old adages "Haste
  makes waste" and "Look before you leap"? They apply to business.

- Follow your strengths and interests. They will sustain your enthusiasm. If
  you like cooking, but hate bookkeeping, hire a bookkeeper so you can do
  what you like to do. After all, one reason to go into business is to be able
  to exercise your favorite skills and interests. Listen to yourself (never easy,
  but always necessary) and be honest. If you don't like being in charge, or
  being responsible, or taking risks, don't try to start a your own restaurant. Instead, work in someone else's restaurant.

- Don't be too proud to quit. If your idea doesn't feel right, don't press on
  just because you don't want to quit. You may be able to modify the start-
  up plan, or switch to another type of restaurant, or overcome whatever
  doesn't feel right. That's fine. There's a big difference between being per-
  sistent and being pigheaded. If the idea continues to raise more doubts
  and worries, it may not be the right idea for you, or the right time to pursue it. Be prepared to abandon your idea if the facts tell you it makes
  sense not to continue. Part of the value of planning is that it reveals warning signals.

There are no road maps to starting a successful restaurant. There are no
shortcuts, either. However, if you pay attention to your personal goals and
desires, make sure your business goals reflect them, and proceed carefully,
you will greatly increase your chances for success.

Cafe Borgia

Karen Jesso

5020 South Lake Shore Drive

#3217 North

Chicago, IL 60615

Phone: 312-288-1993 Fax: 312-2881-995

Dear Professor Rainsford,

You are doing a great service to potential restaurant owners. After completing my M.A. at University of Chicago (Behavioral Sciences), I enrolled in their MBA program. I was surrounded, smothered, and rejected by classmates who dreamed of becoming corporate robots. Fifty thousand dollars later I realized that I had gotten my most important "schooling" while working my way through school as a dishwasher, busgirl, waitress, or bartendress.

I originally met my husband back in 1978 at my little carry-out pizzeria (ironically, the same building that our Cafe is in today). He was six years younger than I. One Saturday it got to be so busy that I couldn't cook all of the pizzas. I said, "Mike! We have to stop deliveries tonight. Tell the customers that they have to come in and pick their pizzas up. You have to help me cook."

It normally takes six months to really train a pizza cook, especially back then when we didn't have very modern equipment. He was like an octopus—making pizzas like I couldn't believe.

When I moved 20 miles away to the University of Chicago campus, I sold my business, but purchased the building that housed the pizzeria and had a small rental apartment unit in back. The building paid for itself, with the small profit I made from the sale of the business.

I told Mike, "I am going to school so I will have to take a job as a waitress somewhere. I know that you are having trouble finishing high school. BUT—please DO FINISH HIGH SCHOOL AND GO TO CHEF SCHOOL— YOU ARE A NATURAL IN THE KITCHEN."

Two years later, Mike manipulated the operator to give him my unlisted phone number. He phoned and informed, "I cannot thank you enough for your taking an interest in my future. Please come with me tonight to McCormick Place. I have competed in the NRA chef competition and finished third in the nation. I'm going to be interviewed on national T.V."

Since then the Cafe has been on television many times. It has also been featured in *Bon Appetit* magazine, *Chicago* magazine, *Inside Chicago* magazine, *Chicago Tribune*, etc.

We opened the Cafe with a $35,000 line of credit—that's the only major time that the University of Chicago MBA came in handy. We tripped over rats in Chicago's restaurant row neighborhood to get equipment. We bought mismatched plates from the flea markets—which ironically got major media approval and recognition.

Mike is responsible for the menu and kitchen, and I manage the dining room hiring and training. However, I put my time in the kitchen just like Mike has hours as host in the dining room. We are both able to empathize with the position of the other's territory.

We prefer to hire people with zero training—it is often easier to teach new habits than to break bad habits. We have a crew of 15 people—eight members of our crew have been with us for over seven out of 10 years.

Cafe Borgia, continued

Our Cafe is about 2,000 square feet and we average 150 customers a day. Our staff is our family. Every year Mike goes to Europe with a different crew member (as a bonus) on a very stimulating culinary excursion. Bonuses are given for consistency with high volume.

I cannot stress to you the importance of telling people to take time in their business plan—our projections were so close to the actual that the banker was amazed.

Also, please tell people not to spend all of their money on the walls—give the money to the crew so that they will be motivated to produce in a profitable manner.

Location—I used $3,000 back in 1978 (money that I had earned baby-sitting) to eventually purchase my property listed for $45,000. My mom almost disowned me stating, "Karen, you don't know a thing about real estate."

I knew enough to realize that the property was on a state highway, three blocks away from I-94, and 20 minutes away from downtown Chicago. I was there one year before McDonald's and Burger King would follow my lead. Even though the building was a run-down shack—LOCATION—LOCATION—LOCATION!!!

The property (excluding business value) according to last year's MAI appraisal was almost $200,000.

Anyway, I hope that I am not boring you, I know that you have other responses to get to. However, I cannot stress to you the importance of your research. Keep me posted on your progress.

Sincerely,

Karen Jesso

TWO

One Year to Nine Months Before Start-Up

TO PROVIDE THE BEST LAUNCHING FOR YOUR RESTAURANT, start to keep track of your thoughts a year or so before start up. A three-ring loose-leaf notebook is a good format, since you will want to rethink some of the ideas you'll grapple with over the next several months, make changes, and keep track of the way these changes are made. Don't trust your memory. As Lao-Tse put it, the finest memory is not so firm as faded ink.

The point of this exercise is to ask yourself questions, write down your answers, and move on. The process is self-correcting—that is, you will change your answers as you go along. Starting a restaurant is such an intriguing activity that this process is a lot of fun. Your ideas change, you change, and your business will ultimately be the better for it.

Ideas come from a number of sources. It is important to choose from more than one potential type of restaurant, in part to protect yourself from a hasty decision and in part because the more you look around and think about possible markets to enter the more ideas you will generate. According to *Inc.* (January 1993, pp. 72*ff*), great ideas come from peer groups, mentors, visits to other companies, your own personalized "textbook" (in which you put clippings and jot down notes and ideas as they come along), industry conferences, competitors, customers, and company suggestion boxes and databases. More routine but perhaps more accessible ideas come from your own experience and observations, reading, travel, and in general keeping your eyes open for restaurant concepts which you think you might be interested in.

Evaluating the ideas you come up with involves more than a feasibility analysis. You have to decide the type of restaurant you want to run. A coffee shop serving breakfast and lunch is a completely different business than a gourmet dinner house—yet both are restaurants. Lifestyle considerations are important too, particularly if you plan to put your family to work.

Much of the evaluating process works by elimination—does this idea fit? does it meet my criteria? The more explicit you are about your selection criteria the better your final choice will be.

Refine Your Ideas

You already have a pretty clear idea of what your restaurant will be. Use the next six months to clarify this picture, make it sharper and better focused, test your assumptions, and improve your general business and restaurant management skills.

Your choice of what kind of restaurant to start is influenced by any number of factors. Some of the more obvious ones include your background, education, and work experience. Less obvious are your answers to questions such as: Whom do you want for customers and clients? What hours do you want to work? How hard do you want to work? How much money do you want/need to earn? What are your long-term goals? The type of restaurant you decide to open (full-service family style, full-service fine dining, quick service, cafeteria, etc.) will have an impact on the types of guests, the hours of operation, the level of culinary and service skills needed, the number of employees, and the potential profitability of your restaurant business.

Note that at this point you can choose what type of restaurant you'll own. Once you have invested substantial cash and effort, your choices will be much narrower, so at this time you should try to make sure that the restaurant you want to start is indeed the right one for you. The "I am going to get rich quick by doing something I don't like doing" attitude leads to failure. Choosing to start a restaurant that reflects your interests and personal goals, on the other hand, is far more rewarding.

Decide the Type of Restaurant You Want to Start

Weigh your choice against your resources, experience, and expectations. Successful start ups depend on a good balance of resources and owner experience. Ask yourself these kinds of questions and jot down your answers:

- *How much money can I invest?* Restaurants, especially during the start-up period, run on cash. Most restaurants are started with a combination of savings and "house money," augmented by trade credit and, in some but not all cases, bank debt and outside investment. The cash you invest becomes permanent capital in the business. The amount required will vary from one type of restaurant to another and will depend to some degree on your depth of experience. Extensive experience can sometimes lower the need for direct capital investment. Short experience requires greater capital to provide a margin for the inevitable errors made during start up.

- *Can (and should) I attract other investors?* Even if you have enough cash to avoid involving other investors, don't automatically go it alone. You may want to have other investors in order to get a strong management team, acquire specific skills, or otherwise bolster your chances of success. Against this, investors want some degree of control, and while this is negotiable to some degree, it isn't always to your best interest to involve these outsiders.

- *What do I do well?* Most of us tend to be good at only a few of the tasks that running a restaurant requires. You might be strong in sales and weak at finance, or terrific at managing people but hopeless at marketing. Knowing your strengths and weaknesses helps you balance your business better. You will want to hire people with the specific skills you lack (or rent their skills on an as-needed basis) in order to concentrate on doing what you do best.

- *What do I like to do?* About the best tip-off to what you do best is to look at what you like to do. What have you enjoyed doing in the past? Do you like to initiate actions, or do you prefer to follow a clear set of directions? Do you prefer to do things yourself, or do you like to delegate and control?

One of the great things about your own business is that you can often set it up to allow you to do what you like to do most—and minimize the time spent doing things you loathe. That doesn't mean that you won't have to do a lot of things that aren't fun. Wait until you have to fire an employee (a task you can't delegate). But, on balance, you will have more control over how you spend your time and effort than you would working in somebody else's restaurant.

The key concept here is that you will work harder, longer, and with more enjoyment at work that interests you. Work that you don't like will, over time, be done grudgingly and perhaps less thoroughly than it should be. The ultimate cost to your business will be higher than it would be if you knew in the first place what you don't like to do, then paid someone else to do those tasks.

- *What would I like to be doing five years from now?* A five-year horizon is useful as a defining tool. In five years you might wish to open another restaurant, expand your existing restaurant, or become a restaurant design consultant. Whatever. Use the five-year test to help understand what you like to do. If you're working towards a goal (not necessarily financial, though financial goals are important, too), the day-to-day frustrations of small-business life are easier to handle. The five-year horizon also helps you define some benchmarks and a plan for attaining them. Maybe you want to be able to spend more time with your family, do community work, or some other non-business activity. Fine. The ability to pursue such goals through building your own business is one of the most potent and satisfying motivators imaginable. Purely business goals ("make a million dollars and retire at the age of 40") tend to be poor motivators, and in the long run unsatisfying. So you make a million dollars. Then what? Make two million? Ten? We bet you won't retire. Building a business is too much fun.

- *What kind of return do I want?* Some businesses are inherently limited in potential, while others have a chance for unlimited growth. Much of the potential depends on you. Debbie Fields turned a cookie store (usually local and limited) into a very large enterprise. Ben and Jerry's Ice Cream began in a garage. The business ideas (make a better cookie, make tastier ice cream) could have led, in different hands, to dwarfed businesses.

- *Some types of restaurants are more profitable than others.* Some of the differences in profitability are due to differences in management ability, others are due to differences in the type of restaurant. The National Restaurant Association statistics show that the average annual unit sales for full-service restaurants are about $500,000 and about $475,000 for limited-service (fast food) restaurants. The National Restaurant Association statistics also show that the average income before income taxes is about 4.2 percent for full-service restaurants and 9.0 percent for quick-service restaurants. Thus, the average before tax profit for full-service restaurants is $21,000 per year ($500,000 x 4.2 percent) and $42,750 per year ($475,000 x 9.0 percent) for quick service restaurants. (If you doubted our comment in Chapter One that you probably won't get rich overnight in the restaurant business, then these figures should eliminate those doubts.)

- *How will I get out of the business?* It's never too early to begin thinking about an exit strategy. Sooner or later you'll come to a point at which you have to leave the day to day operations. There are numerous options: leave feet first, shut the restaurant down, sell it, pass it along to children or employees, or merge it into a bigger operation. Some restaurant ventures are started with the idea that they will "go public" in a short time, allowing the founders to start other ventures. This is rare in the restaurant business, but not unheard of.

Whatever your strategy will eventually be, if you plan from the outset to run your restaurant as if you were going to sell it, you'll run it more profitably than if you just run it on a day to day basis. One of the best tax shelters is to start a business, run it for a profit, and then sell it for a multiple of earnings. Correction: this is *the* best tax shelter.

Use "Constructive Daydreaming" to Set Business Goals that Are Consistent with Your Personal Goals

Daydreams play an interesting and important role in starting a business. First, the initial idea to start a business often comes in the form of a daydream: What if I had started Outback or East Side Mario's? What would it be like to run that business? I know I could improve on this business—here's what I'd do.

Second, constructive daydreaming is a terrific technique to try out the fit between business goals and personal goals. The aim here is to form a sketch of your business which can be filled in as you go along. Imagine going to the restaurant every day. What are you doing? How does it feel? What do you do when you aren't at the office? And so on. Your restaurant is going to be an extension of your own personality no matter how hard you try to make it something else, so it makes good sense to look ahead. If the picture doesn't feel right, chances are excellent that there is a disparity between what you want to do and what the restaurant, as you project it, makes you do. You'll have plenty of compromises to make without setting the stage for long-term, self-defeating behavior. Running a business to achieve goals you don't like is stupid. Projecting the future doesn't determine the future, but it does help you twist the odds in your favor.

Assess the Impact on Your Family and Personal Life

Starting a restaurant affects every facet of your life. There are always loose ends to tie up, work to do, and bills to pay. Also, you probably will be working in your restaurant nights and weekends when other people are playing. The result is that your family and social life will suffer. A supportive family and understanding friends go a long way to making your restaurant a success.

The emotional ups and downs inherent in a start-up are unexpected and often severe. You'll find that periods of elation and excitement are followed by panic when accounts receivable are slow to turn into cash, or a supplier pulls out, or a weekend snowstorm results in not a single customer. If you are not used to the fluctuating fortunes of restaurant ownership, be aware. This is a problem that you will have to learn to live with. Corporate refugees find this especially tough to swallow.

Make sure you consider how your new venture will affect your:

- *Income.* Unless you are able to retain your full-time job and hire someone to run your restaurant (a scenario we definitely do not recommend), your income will suffer. Start-up businesses almost never provide a decent salary to the owner right away. If you can, save some money to plug this gap. A second income—a supportive spouse or significant other—can also make a big difference.

- *Hours.* Start-ups devour time. In the first few months of a business, when everything is new and shortcuts haven't been discovered, you'll literally live your business. You'll think about it all the time, whether at the restaurant or not. Your time will not be your own—one of the biggest problems newcomers to restaurant ownership face is that they

Ron Bock

Loco Perro Restaurant

191 E. High St. East Hampton, CT 06424

860-267-2945

Most people have no idea how much time is involved in running a successful restaurant. They have this TV image of greeting guests, overseeing a cooperative and educated staff of dedicated employees, mingling with customers and making huge sums of money. Not!

Those are the restaurants that promptly go out of business. This has been called the toughest business in the world with the highest failure rate. The average profit is 4.3 percent! That's 4.3 cents on the dollar and there are hundreds of ways to lose that 4.3 cents; just accept an American Express card and you lose money! (They charge 4.8 percent of every sale they process; we do not accept American Express.) Successful restaurateurs work 80–90 hours a week as their NORMAL week! In the beginning they work well over 100 hours a week. They bring an extra change of clothes to work because they know the first set will be dirty by 4 P.M., from cleaning something, fixing something or spilling something. They will know or learn every job in the business from cleaning toilets, washing dishes, cooking, bartending and waiting table to hosting and dealing with customer complaints. The customer is ALMOST always right even when they are idiots, and there are plenty of idiots. Remember we're dealing in volume in this business. In a successful restaurant you are probably the first one in, in the morning and the last one to leave at night!

OK so why would anyone get into this business!? I ask myself this lots of times. It becomes YOUR LIFE NOT A JOB! If you think you're going to work a 40 hour week in this business, just flush all your money down the toilet now! It will save you a lot of time, headaches, heartaches and heartbreak. You will spend more time at your restaurant then you ever do at home. You will eat, sleep and think about what you can do to improve it or change it everywhere you go. It is also one of the most creative outlets you will ever find. You control the menu, the atmosphere, the staff, the music, the 1,000's of little details that make the whole show work! And that's exactly what it is, "A SHOW." It's a production you prepare every day and perform every night. It's entertainment! People can eat at home to save money. When people go out it's an experience. Even if it's a formal restaurant it's still entertainment. It's the ambiance, the music, the lighting, the food, the service, it's a SHOW. People will come in and say "you know what you should do here?" and then proceed to tell you their one idea that you already thought of and tried three years ago. You bite your tongue and try to be pleasant. There is no ONE THING that makes a restaurant successful! It's hundreds of things all working together. Most restaurateurs are extremely creative people and that's why we are in this business because the hours and pay stink but the creative rewards are very fulfilling. It's great to hear people tell you how much they love your restaurant.

I have enclosed a portion of our menu that you may find of interest. Good luck with your book. Maybe you could write one on how to be a good customer, a lot of people could use it. Unfortunately, they don't know they need it. Please forgive typos and spelling, no time to check it, have to get back to work, the dishwasher just broke down again and we're out of ice for margaritas and the bartender just called in sick.........ADIOS AMIGO.

Ron Bock a.k.a. Jack Trevor

can't forget the business at 5 o'clock and go home. They lug the restaurant home with them. So will you.

- *Support level.* Wholehearted support from family and friends helps you avoid burnout. People who take an intelligent interest in your restaurant can provide you with objective advice and criticism. To get this kind of support, keep them informed from the start. Don't keep everything to yourself. If you are worried, tell them. If you are uncertain, tell them.

The loneliness that goes with restaurant ownership is self-induced. Somehow the myth of the rugged individual who never shows the least sign of doubt or fear has become mixed up with being the owner. Don't buy the myth. Your family and friends have a sizable emotional investment in you and your business. Let them help, and they will. Give them a return on their investment and all of you benefit. They will understand the demands of your restaurant better, which in turn defuses their concerns about the amount of time, effort, and worry you put into your start up.

- *Commitment to family, community, personal activities.* Many restaurateurs find that the lack of time for family, community, and personal activities (hobbies, sports, reading, and so on) is the highest price they pay for restaurant ownership. During the start-up period this price is reasonable. Later, when the business is actually going, it becomes a leading cause of burnout. At this point, make sure you have a clear picture of what your commitments will be, how long they'll take to fulfill, and what sacrifices (if any) you'll have to make.

Some other considerations you should have:

- Some restaurants are more limiting than others. Most restaurants demand that the owner be there all the time. The hours are long, the rewards high—but it may not be a good choice for a person who places a premium on family or community activities. Seasonal restaurants or a city restaurant catering to the business luncheon clientele will probably consume less time.

- A shaky marriage or other relationship is never improved by starting a business (or buying one). Don't expect to lose yourself in your start up and magically come out of it with a better marriage.

- Starting your restaurant should be a positive and exciting experience. Negative motivations don't last. Positive motivations do, which is why it is so important that you place your personal goals ahead of your business goals. Your restaurant should serve your goals.

Begin Your Research

Information sources come in two varieties: "hot" and "cool." You will need both kinds. "Hot" information sources are interpersonal. Hot information is

O ne of our survey respondents had this advice for you:

"My advice to those who want to open a restaurant:

If you aren't going to be there, don't do it!

If you don't know what level of sales it will take to retire your debt, don't do it!

If you think the restaurant business is easy, don't do it!

Your opening costs will be higher than you think.

Pay the bank first (after you pay the government)!

KEEP IT SIMPLE STUPID!

P.S. If available, I would be the best operations/cost control advisor you will ever know! Best of luck!

interpersonal, interactive, and provides immediate feedback. "Cool" information sources are less interactive, and for many entrepreneurs less fun. Reading, observing, and attending lectures are good examples of cool information. Although these activities are not too interactive, they have high information value for the time invested.

Get Hot Information

Work in management in your chosen type of restaurant. While this is not always a possible option, you can't beat it for value. You can learn the tricks of the trade, the jargon, and when and where problems tend to crop up. You get to know suppliers, customers, and how to keep the guests happy. And you get paid while doing so. Almost as good as this is working in a non-management position. While your experience won't be as broad, it will be direct and immediately valuable.

Talk with people already in the restaurant business. Ask a lot of questions of current and former owners: What's different about your restaurant? What's good or bad about it? What's the future? What kinds of problems do you encounter? What's your biggest headache? We hope we've helped you with this process by providing you with the sidebars in this *Guide* which summarize the results of our survey of restaurateurs.

Seek out the names of experts and other helpful hot information sources. If you structure a list of questions, you can make sure that you don't impose on their time, and you enhance the value of the information you receive. Figure 2.1 gives you an idea of some of the questions you should be asking. Keep notes. Hot information melts away if you don't write it down.

Some other hot information sources are:

- *Businesses in non-competitive locations*. Take a trip and seek out other restaurant owners. Tell them what you're up to and point out that you won't be competing. The magic phrase "I've got a problem and I think you can help me" opens many doors. You will always get a better reception if you make an appointment, tell them how long it will take, and submit a list of questions (see Figure 2.1) that you will ask. In fact, this is a good technique for anyone whom you would like to interview, since it puts some boundaries on the visit and gives the individual a chance to prepare.

- *Competitors*. Your competitors may be willing to talk with you. Try them. The worst they can do is tell you lies. Use your judgment.

Figure 2.1: Sample Questions

These are questions we tend to ask. You don't have to follow every bit of advice, and cannot since it will often be inconsistent. Your goal is to become aware of what tricks of the trade you should know.

➤ What were your main start-up problems? What special problems did you have after a year in business?

➤ If you knew then what you know now, what would you have done differently?

➤ How long does it take to get trade credit? What do suppliers look for? Who are the most reliable suppliers?

➤ What are the best information sources for a restaurant like this?

➤ What kind of mark up/margins/gross profit should I expect during my start up year?

➤ What kind of computers and point-of-sale (POS) equipment do you use? Why? What would you recommend that I use?

➤ What trade associations do you find valuable?

➤ What kind of training should I get? What should I provide to employees?

➤ Are there any special problems in the restaurant business I should look out for?

➤ What do you like best (dislike most) about being in the restaurant business?

- *Attend trade shows.* Don't miss this one. Trade shows are a great hot information source. Many of the suppliers and consultants to the industry will be there. The National Restaurant Association trade show is held in Chicago every May, but many state or city restaurant associations hold regional shows annually.

- *Trade association executives and editors, consultants to the industry, persons who finance the industry (include local bankers), and career counselors in the industry.* Anyone with direct connections to the restaurant industry may have useful insights. Make sure to get in touch with these people.

- *Federal, state, and university programs.* Start with the Small Business Administration (SBA) programs. The SBA is listed in the white pages of your phone book under the general heading United States Government. Their web site is http://www.sbaonline.sba.gov. The SBA is the entry point for a number of excellent programs including SCORE (Service Corps of Retired Executives) and SBDCs (Small Business Development Centers).

- *SCORE* (Service Corps of Retired Executives) programs provide management seminars and direct business consulting services. The SCORE counselors are experienced business people, some of whom are terrific at helping you get a business up and going. The ACE (Active Corps of Executives) program is similar, except that the counselors are still active in business.

- *SBDCs* (Small Business Development Centers) are usually attached to universities. If you have an SBDC available, make full use of it. Their expertise and willingness to help are especially useful when it comes time to write your business plan. They provide direct consulting services and are a most effective link to other sources of information and assistance. Their mission is to strengthen the small business community, including your business.

- *Local college and university business school faculty.* Many are involved with small business in one way or another and can steer you to specific programs and experts.

- *Your state commissioner of economic development.* You pay a lot of taxes; this is a chance to get a return on your investment. Some communities have local economic development or business development officers. Call your Secretary of State in your state's capital and ask him or her for help.

- *Your local chamber of commerce.* Chambers act as a clearinghouse for a number of programs and will give you directions whether you are a member or not.

Get Cool Information

Books, lectures, and other low-interactive activities tend to be more solitary and analytic than hot information sources, but don't ignore their value. In the trade, these are called "secondary sources."

Start with your local librarian. He or she will help organize and plan your research. If you have a business library or a business school library nearby, pay it a visit and ask for help. Your research should include:

- *The Small Business Sourcebook* published by Gale Research. It includes over 45 pages of restaurant information sources, including trade associations, publications, financial data sources, and a bibliography that is updated annually

- Trade publications, especially periodicals

- National Restaurant Association publications

- Government publications, including the wide range of low-cost SBA publications available through district SBA offices, local SCORE, and ACE programs, and by mail

- Check the Resources list in Appendix C of this *Guide*

Set up clip files to organize the information you gather. Manila folders and some paper and pencils are all you need. Take notes on those articles or books you can't clip. The database you build over a period of a few weeks saves you months of work later on. A lot of basic demographic and market research can be gleaned from magazines and journals. Once more, ask your librarian for help.

You could also subscribe to a data base or clipping service such as RSVP/FIND in New York. This is a cost-effective option if you need very extensive, very up-to-date information, or information that is hard to locate. However, these services can be expensive.

Build Your Skills by Taking Formal Management Courses

Formal management courses are a fast way up the learning curve if you've had little management experience. Remember: There is no prize given for reinventing standard management practices which have evolved over years of painstaking effort by millions of intelligent people.

- *Attend a SCORE Pre-business Workshop.* This one's a must. A pre-business workshop helps you with your business plan. Its greatest value may be in the interaction with other people facing the same start-up fears and concerns. Call SCORE and ask when their next pre-business seminar takes place. The cost is trivial. The payoff is immense.

You also will get a chance to meet your local SCORE chapter counselors. They can be a strong source of information and direct, hands-on consulting. A word of caution, however: Make sure the counselor you'll be working with has experience with your type of business.

- *Check with the nearest Small Business Development Center (SBDC).* SBDCs run seminars for small businesses and participate in

The restaurateurs in our survey indicated that "gut reaction" and other restaurateurs were the most important sources for gathering information. We suspect that by "gut reaction" they meant that when they saw something they liked—either when they were doing their research or years before—they either wrote it down or made a mental note. That's fine, but we suggest you write it down so you don't forget. That's part of doing research for your restaurant: seeing what others are doing.

We also urge you to make more use of the World Wide Web (WWW) which wasn't available when many of our restaurateurs started up—remember, they have been in business for an average of almost 15 years! It's cheap, easy to use once you get the hang of it, time saving, and extensive. Besides searching out the websites for the National Restaurant Association and other trade organizations, you can check out other restaurants all over the country.

How important were each of the following resources for gathering data in the planning stages of your restaurant?

	"1"	"2"	"3"	"4"	"5"	Avg.
"Gut reaction?"	1.2%	6.1%	18.3%	40.2%	34.1%	4.0
Other restaurateurs?	10.7%	20.2%	33.3%	28.6%	7.1%	3.0
"How to" books?	36.1%	30.1%	20.5%	7.2%	6.0%	2.2
Government agencies?	34.9%	39.8%	18.1%	6.0%	1.2%	2.0
Consultants?	46.4%	26.2%	17.9%	6.0%	3.6%	1.9
Data bases (WWW)?	47.6%	28.0%	17.1%	4.9%	2.4%	1.9

"1" = Not Important
"2" = Slightly Important
"3" = Important
"4" = Very Important
"5" = Extremely Important

business association programs run by other groups. Their help is direct, hands-on, and usually one-on-one.

- *Find out about SBA-sponsored seminars and short courses.* The SBA sponsors numerous short, intensive, problem-specific courses including one for people planning to start businesses. Again, make sure the course meets your needs.

- *Check with local colleges for extension programs.* Include vocational and technical schools; they often provide down-to-earth seminars and workshops.

- *Look into programs sponsored by trade associations,* often found at trade shows or in conjunction with regional business expositions. You don't have to be a member of the trade association to attend these. Just get on the mailing list by subscribing to the trade magazine for your kind of business.

- *Find out about business expositions sponsored by business groups. Inc.* Magazine has an annual "growing the business" seminar series. Business associations such as SBANE (Small Business Association of New England) put on programs in major cities every year. Some of the larger chambers of commerce sponsor local programs.

- *Become familiar with "high tech" solutions to problems in the restaurant business.* No intelligent restaurant owner should try to run his or her business without taking full advantage of the microcomputer revolution. If you are not computer literate, become computer literate and comfortable as soon as possible. The more familiar you are with using the computer the better. You should also learn to use a modem to access public and trade databases. The amount of information out there is unbelievable—and immensely valuable to you.

Along the same line, an "intelligent cash register" will pay for itself very quickly. A point-of-sale (POS) terminal will provide you with both efficiency and valuable data for analyzing your restaurant business.

Use the year before starting your business to visualize and flesh out a picture of your business, including its impact on your personal life. Take skill-building courses and conduct basic research to increase the odds in your favor. This includes both interactive and solitary research. Become aware of and utilize the many federal and state programs that have been established to help you successfully start your own business. And don't fail to take your local librarian out to lunch: his or her skills are highly professional, seldom called upon by business owners, and extraordinarily helpful to you in this research phase of your start up.

Chapter Two Action Plan

A. Concept Development (Type of Restaurant, Theme, Decor, Type of Service, etc.)

Action/Strategy	Target Date	Person Responsible	Results/ Comments
1. Start a three-ring notebook labeled "Concept Development."			
2. Start to gather data about different types of restaurants.			
3. Do preliminary research about the type of competition you will be facing. How many total restaurants? What type of restaurants? Where do there seem to be voids in the market place?			
4. Visit other restaurants. Which seem to be popular and busy? Why? Which seem to be struggling? Why?			
5. Interview restaurateurs about concept development issues to consider.			
6. Start a preliminary search for locations. Are sites available to lease? To buy?			
Add your own actions/strategies here.			

Action Plan, continued

B. Financial Issues (Pro Forma Income Statements, Cash Flow Statements, Balance Sheets, etc.)

Action/Strategy	Target Date	Person Responsible	Results/ Comments
1. Start a three-ring notebook labeled "Financial Issues."			
2. Interview restaurateurs about concept financial issues to consider.			
3. Begin to put together rough financial statements.			
4. Begin to investigate potential sources for obtaining debt and equity funds.			
5. Investigate potential costs for leasing, buying, or constructing your restaurant.			
6. Familiarize yourself with the *Uniform System of Accounts for Restaurants* and start to build computerized spreadsheets for future "what if" scenarios.			
Add your own actions/strategies here.			

Action Plan, continued

C. Operational Issues (Menu, Kitchen Design, Work Flow, Patron Flow, etc.)

Action/Strategy	Target Date	Person Responsible	Results/ Comments
1. Start a three-ring notebook labeled "Operational Issues."			
2. Interview restaurateurs about concept and operational issues to consider.			
3. Think about optimal size and square footage requirements for kitchen, storage, dining, and lounge areas.			
4. Begin a file of standardized recipes.			
5. Contact new and used restaurant equipment dealers.			
Add your own actions/strategies here.			

Action Plan, continued

D. Legal Issues (Legal Entity, Permits and Licenses, State and Federal Income and Personal Taxes, etc.)

Action/Strategy	Target Date	Person Responsible	Results/ Comments
1. Start a three-ring notebook labeled "Legal Issues."			
2. Interview restaurateurs about concept legal issues to consider.			
3. Start to get information about lawyers, insurance agents, and accountants who could serve your needs.			
4. Get information about obtaining health permits, liquor licenses, and other necessary permits.			
5. Get information about insurance requirements and liability insurance.			
6. Begin to think about the business entity (sole proprietorship, partnership, corporation, or limited liability corporation) most appropriate for your needs.			
Add your own actions/strategies here.			

Action Plan, continued

E. Personal Issues

Action/Strategy	Target Date	Person Responsible	Results/ Comments
1. Start a three-ring notebook labeled "Personal Issues."			
2. List the reasons you would like to start your own restaurant.			
3. Discuss your reasons with family and friends.			
4. Interview restaurateurs about concept personal issues to consider.			
5. Make an inventory of your general management and restaurant management skills.			
6. Make a plan for further developing your general management skills.			
7. Make a plan for further developing your restaurant management skills.			
8. Develop a better understanding of the restaurant industry.			
9. Update your computer skills.			
10. Find the National Restaurant Association's web page and make a bookmark so you can access it easily.			
Add your own actions/strategies here.			

THREE

Nine to Six
Months Before Start-Up

Determine Your Restaurant Concept

The key start-up question is: What business are you really in? Your answer will influence all of your business plans and will affect your perception of your markets. This in turn will determine what kinds of research will pay off best for you, what groups to join or ally yourself with, and where to locate your restaurant.

The immediate impulse is to say "I'm in the restaurant business" or "I sell good food and service to a luncheon crowd." These are beginnings of answers, built on products or markets. The aim is to define what business you are in, what you really sell and to whom, and what makes your business different—all in 25 words or less. You will use the resulting mission statement or company motto to keep your business focused on its primary business. One of the biggest pitfalls for new restaurants is to be unclear about the thrust of the business. As a result, efforts are scattered and fragmentary, many expensive and distracting false starts are made, and all too often the fledgling business is crippled.

Mission Statements

A good mission statement will help determine what you should do. It will address the question, "What business should you be in?" This may or may not be the business that you are in. Your mission statement should answer these questions: Who is your market (or: Who are your customers)? What is your product or service—and what benefits does it provide your market? What is your special competence or strength or competitive advantage? Your mission statement should ideally be based on an "environmental scan" in which you look at the internal strengths and weaknesses of the business as well as the opportunities and threats presented by the various environments within which the business operates. This "SWOT" analysis—

Figure 3.1: Mission Statement Worksheet

Write down a few words about your restaurant in each of the following categories. Write down the single most important goal for your business. Then condense the result into one or two short sentences. This will result in a mission statement that accurately reflects your restaurant's purposes.

Customers:

downtown community

tourists (during summer and fall)

young adults

special events

Products or Services:

weekend brunch, luncheons and dinners

great burgers, salads and seafood

"comfort foods" for young adults

pasta and limited Mexican items

locally grown produce in season

full bar with a many different beers on tap & in bottle

Markets:

primarily the weekday lunch and dinner crowd: young adults and downtown workers

after work crowd from downtown

Economic Objectives:

make a profit, stable revenues

Beliefs, Values and Aspirations:

provide consistently good food and excellent service

provide a pleasant gathering place for young adults (21 to 35, more or less)

Distinctive Competence: What are we *really* good at?

excellent service, fast and courteous

fresh, appealing moderately priced food

clean and attractive premises (think of McDonald's for cleanliness!)

a truly great bartender

Concern for Employees:

courteous, well-trained waitstaff and other employees are the key to our success

Goals:

to make a profit

to provide a gathering place for the 21 to 35 market

Mission Statement:

We will continue to profitably provide fast, courteous service in congenial surroundings to the downtown worker and young adult markets. Our menu, complemented by a wide array of local and specialty beers, is tailored to their tastes and budgets.

Strengths, Weaknesses, Opportunities, and Threats—helps keep you from being blindsided by changes in technology, regulation, competition and so on, and should be part of your ongoing duties. See Figure 3.1.

Start with Your Market

Who will you be selling to? Always place the customer (actual or prospective) at the center of your strategies. If you don't have customers, you don't have a business.

One of the biggest benefits of a start-up restaurant is that you have some latitude in determining who your guests will be. All things being equal, it's better to deal with people you like, respect, and are comfortable with than with people you dislike, look down upon, or are uncomfortable with. Your realistic target markets need what you plan to sell, are accessible to you (through advertising and other promotional means as well as through your location), and have some reason to buy from you rather than from your competitors. There have to be enough of them to make your venture a profitable one. You should know a lot about your markets, which is a function of your experience and familiarity with them.

Keep in mind that all buying decisions are made by individuals, and are ultimately subjective. For this reason alone, your chances of success are enhanced by your familiarity with people in your target markets. If you don't know them, make sure you know somebody who does. Few things are less rewarding and more costly than selling into markets you know little or nothing about.

Definition: *Markets* are those persons or organizations who will be your customers, while target markets are those persons or organizations most likely to become your customers. *Target markets* are small and tightly defined. A common start-up error is to assume that everyone is a prospective customer. Everyone is not. Your markets are limited by geography, age, education, income and other demographic factors, competition, your skill at promoting and advertising your business, and dozens of other factors. And even your target markets will have different subgroups of greater or lesser value to you. Think of a bull's eye (most valuable prospects) versus outer rings (less valuable prospects) on an archery target. You want to focus on the bull's eye and not squander your efforts and resources trying to reach less likely prospects.

Choose Your Menu and Service Level

Your menu and service will ideally be chosen with your prospective customers (target markets) in mind. What can you offer your markets that they are ready and eager to buy? Start ups which try to educate their markets to something brand new and different are rarely successful. Leave education to large, established businesses.

Give serious consideration to these questions:

- What are the menu items and level of service you plan to offer?

- How will your target markets find out about you?

- Why would your target markets patronize your restaurant?

- When will they buy them? Days of the week? Hours of the day?

- How will they pay: cash or credit?

- What price range are you going to offer?

- Where are they going to eat your food? On-premises or off-premises?

Notice that these questions all have marketing components. Every decision you make in your business should include consideration of your markets. For example, the National Restaurant Association research indicates that off-premise consumption amounted for almost half of all restaurant traffic in 1994. Thus, you had better give serious consideration to take-out and/or drive through capabilities. If you forget your customers, your customers will forget you. Fast. And remember that without customers, you don't have a business.

Determine What Makes You Different

What will set you apart from your competitors?

Differentiation (or positioning) is arguably the most important small business marketing strategy. Your aim is to locate a market niche, a market large enough to be profitable, small enough to defend against other businesses, and suited to your resources, interests, and abilities.

Some differentiating ideas will fit your start up. Others won't. You want to decide ahead of time how you wish to position your business so you can influence your markets' perceptions of your business. If you plan to sell on quality, you will go one way. If you decide to differentiate your business on grounds of convenience, or price, or speed of service, you have other

When deciding on a concept, the restaurateurs in our survey indicated that if you don't have the money—or a way to get it—don't even bother going any further. Financing aside, consumer preferences, the competitive situation, and demographic trends all rated high. These views reinforce our point that you need to develop a concept that the market will support (just because you like something doesn't mean lots of other people do) and one where the competition is not too fierce. Even though pizza is one of the most popular menu items, if there is an over abundance of pizza restaurants in your market area you will face an uphill battle. You're better off developing a concept that is popular but has a lower level of competition—not always an easy combination to find.

Please rate the importance of each of the following when developing a restaurant concept.

	"1"	"2"	"3"	"4"	"5"	Avg.
Availability of capital	0.0%	1.2%	7.1%	36.5%	55.3%	4.5
Consumer preferences	1.2%	4.8%	14.5%	31.3%	48.2%	4.2
Competitive situation	1.2%	9.6%	34.9%	30.1%	24.1%	3.7
Demographic trends	1.2%	20.5%	28.9%	31.3%	18.1%	3.4
Government regulations	4.8%	27.7%	38.6%	16.9%	12.0%	3.0

"1" = Not Important
"2" = Slightly Important
"3" = Important
"4" = Very Important
"5" = Extremely Important

options. You cannot follow all of them without hopelessly blurring your image.

Here are some ways restaurants differentiate their menu items and service levels.

• Quality

• Service

• Perceived value

• Convenience

• Reliability

• Price

• Familiarity

• Native son or daughter

• Product range

• Specialization

As you get more familiar with your markets and competition, you will begin to see other ways to differentiate your restaurant. The important thing is to be careful and consistent. The image your restaurant projects when it starts will be very hard to change later, if it can be changed at all.

Start Writing Your Business Plan

A business plan is a short written document that serves as a guide to your future, provides direction and focus, and helps you model your business and avoid problems. As noted in Chapter Two, avail yourself of SCORE's pre-business workshop to get started on your plan. Most SBDCs run planning workshops several times a year, which may suit your needs better. Also get a copy of Upstart's *Restaurant Planning Guide*, which is described in the Resources section on p. 174.

Your business plan helps you define your financing needs with some accuracy. More important, it makes running your business much easier. The Outline of a Business Plan on p. 32 serves as a guide in alerting you to all the different items your business plan should contain.

Refine Your Initial Mission Statement or Company Motto

What business are you going to be in? Keep working at your answer. It should change as your research progresses. Remember that your aim is to find ways to make your restaurant stand out from others, including both direct and indirect competitors.

Outline of a Business Plan

- Cover Sheet: Name of business, names of principals, address and phone number
- Statement of Purpose
- Table of Contents

SECTION ONE: THE BUSINESS

   A. Description of Business

   B. Product/Service

   C. Market

   D. Location of Business

   E. Competition

   F. Management

   G. Personnel

   H. Application and Expected Effect of Loan (if needed)

   I. Summary

SECTION TWO: FINANCIAL DATA

   A. Sources and Applications of Funding

   B. Capital Equipment List

   C. Balance Sheet

   D. Break-Even Analysis

   E. Income Projections (Profit and Loss Statements)

      1. Three-year summary

      2. Detail by month for first year

      3. Detail by quarter for second and third years

      4. Notes of explanation

   F. Cash Flow Projection

      1. Detail by month for first year

      2. Detail by quarter for second and third years

      3. Notes of explanation

   G. Deviation Analysis

   H. Historical Financial Reports for Existing Business

      1. Balance sheets for past three years

      2. Income statements for past three years

      3. Tax returns

SECTION THREE: SUPPORTING DOCUMENTS

Personal resumes, personal balance sheets, cost of living budget, credit reports, letters of reference, job descriptions, letters of intent, copies of leases, contracts, legal documents, and anything else relevant to the plan.

List Your Strongest Competition

Competition is a fact of business life. If you have no competitors, you probably don't have a viable business idea, or haven't come to grips with what business you are really in. Theodore Levitt, in a classic essay entitled "Marketing Myopia," noted that some years ago Hollywood decided that it was in the movie business, and that television was not competition. After losing billions of dollars of business to this newer medium, Hollywood finally realized that it was in the entertainment business, not just movies, and began to compete successfully.

All businesses have competition. List your five closest direct competitors and begin to collect information on them. Clip copies of their advertisements, jot down notes on your observations of them, pay them visits as a customer. (See Chapter Six, p. 97 on competitor files for a more thorough method.)

You will partially define your restaurant by your competition. You need to define clearly what business your restaurant is in, what markets it will serve, and how it will differentiate itself from other restaurants in the area. If you know who these competitors are and how they attempt to differentiate their place in the market, and how well they are achieving their goals, you can find ways to successfully grab market share.

However, you cannot do this if you don't know your competition thoroughly. The better you know your competition, the better you will be able to compete. Start with the most direct competitors, but keep an eye out for indirect competition, those that aren't obvious competitors. For example, grocery stores now offer ready-to-eat and heat-and-serve food to go. Some even have in-store dining areas.

Your competitor list will grow. Start it early, add to it as needed, and be prepared to receive disproportionate benefits from your research.

Prepare Your Personal Financial Statement

You will need a personal financial statement to obtain financing and trade credit, to set your own compensation, and for financial planning in general.

Your bank has free personal financial statement forms. A cost-of-living budget form is provided in this book's Appendix; it helps you get a grip on what your basic income needs add up to. Make sure to add 30 percent to this figure, since underestimating income needs is a major problem for new business owners. If your income doesn't meet your basic needs, worry and panic set in. If you take out too much, you can strangle your cash flow. Setting a realistic balance is extremely important.

When you work out your personal financial statements and cost-of-living budget, get your spouse (or partner or other family supporters) to go over it with you. The fewer surprises you spring on them, the more supportive they'll be when you need them.

Define Your Target Markets

Defining target markets is another ongoing project. Don't do it once and expect to enjoy success. Your markets change. People move. Tastes change. Competition increases, especially in profitable markets. Products and services change, and what sold yesterday won't sell today.

Eventually, you will almost unconsciously redefine your markets. That takes experience, though, and to offset a lack of experience, be prepared to go through a lot of spadework.

Interview Prospective Customers

You can't beat prospective customers as a source of hot information. Ask yourself who might patronize your restaurant, then interview them. Your SBDC, SCORE, or SBA advisors will help you determine your best markets. Use them. They also can help with surveys and basic market research. (See "Begin Your Research," Chapter Two, p. 15.)

People like to express their opinions. You need to listen to them; this information will help you define what your business will be. People buy what they want to buy, which is not necessarily what you plan to sell.

Visit Similar Restaurants

Restaurants like yours are another important source of information. Visit as many as you can. Who are they selling to? How do they sell? What ways do they use to differentiate themselves?

This kind of research is far superior to armchair research for one major reason: It is current. By the time you read an article or book, the information is dated. That doesn't mean it's valueless—but it does mean that you, as an astute entrepreneur, will want to make sure that your information is still valid.

Restaurant owners you aren't competing with (since they are outside your market area or appeal to a completely different clientele) will share their insights with you if you explain what you are planning, ask their help, and don't impose on their time. Ask your insurance agent when is the best time to make an appointment with these business owners. (Insurance agents have to know these things.)

Important Questions Your Research Should Cover

Whether you're interviewing prospective accountants, meeting new colleagues at a chamber of commerce function, or talking with people from your trade association, make sure to ask:

- How is business in this area—is it growing? Stable?

- What is the economic outlook?

- How many restaurants like mine can this region support?

- What questions should someone in my position be asking?

Research Business and Trade Organizations

Trade and business organizations are another source of valuable information. There are hundreds of state and local restaurant trade associations, so you'll be able to find one that fits the kind of restaurant you plan to start.

Ask Your Librarian for Help

Ask your librarian to help you find trade information on your business. He or she will steer you to *Ayers' Dictionary of Trade Associations* and other listings.

Also ask him or her:

- What your SIC (Standard Industrial Classification) code number is—all government data is listed by SIC number.

- About business census data

- What current general business periodicals you should read

- About trade publications

- For books and other publications specific to the restaurant industry

- What your library can get for you through interlibrary loans

- Some librarians can help you focus a search for electronic information (the Internet, bulletin boards, chat groups for the restaurant industry)

The National Restaurant Association has regional and state chapters. There are also local restaurant associations. Pay yours a visit. Most of them have publications for their members. The information you get is worth the price of membership. It is targeted to your business, is delivered to your mailbox, links you to businesses similar to yours, and provides a forum for asking questions. And you can always call the editor and ask more detailed questions. Editors get paid to spot trends and problems and to answer questions. Use the World Wide Web as well to gather information about the restaurant industry.

Business associations are less focused, but nonetheless valuable as a way to meet other business owners and participate in educational activities. National Small Business United, the National Federation of Independent Businesses, and similar groups offer a wide range of services.

Get In Touch with Your Chamber of Commerce

Join your chamber of commerce. Chambers of commerce provide local information, business education programs, mailing lists, and a chance to rub elbows with other business owners. The last may be the most important, because when you have started your business, you'll have questions that are best answered by people who have successfully answered the same questions.

Local business groups other than the chamber, like certain professional associations, are worth checking out, but are secondary in importance. You won't have a lot of time for these associations when you are in business, though during the pre-start-up period they can provide helpful insights and contacts.

Check your newspaper for listings of local business organizations. You can often find out what's available by calling the business editor; otherwise a few minutes spent looking over the business pages will give you names and addresses of groups that might appeal to you.

Seek the Best Location

Choose the location for your restaurant with great care. Investing time to choose a good location well ahead of start up pays off handsomely.

For the restaurant industry, location is all-important. Making a decision on cost concerns alone is risky. Location and image are so tightly intertwined that the wrong location can undermine an otherwise sound business.

A storefront is vital to a restaurant, in part because it is the most direct channel of distribution between you and your guest. Most restaurants require their customers to come to the restaurant (although Domino's Pizza changed that paradigm and delivery by restaurants is becoming more and more important). Visual appeal is critical to get first-time customers to enter. If guests will be arriving by car, then access and adequate parking are necessary. (Speaking of access,

Dozens of different people have been credited with saying. "Location, location, location," when asked what are the three most important factors for success in the restaurant business (or hotel business or retail business for that matter). It doesn't really matter who said it first, what does matter is that you heed the advice. Location is one of the most critical factors in success.

No, location alone will not insure success—you must also do the other things well in order to succeed. One of our respondents told us:

My restaurant went into a location where four others had failed. I set out to do pizza better than anyone in our area (13 others) and did. A single item menu, "funky" surroundings, great perceived value, and constantly changing the menu at customers' suggestions were how I did it.

Happy Trails,

Cowboy Bob

restaurants located on second floors don't seem to work. You may save a lot of rent but your customer counts may not be enough to pay it, no matter how low it is!) Traffic counts and safety and security issues should also be addressed.

Talk with Realtors, Bankers, and Your Chamber of Commerce

Before settling on a location, consult the people who can help you make a wise choice. Realtors are knowledgeable about markets for commercial property, but talk to more than one and don't rely on them alone. Talk to your banker and other advisors. Bankers provide another viewpoint for evaluating commercial locations and often are aware of trends earlier than other people.

Don't jump at the first good site. Choose from a variety of locations, and take your time. If you decide to rent, remember that leases are negotiable. They are also hard to get out of so be sure to get legal advice before you sign.

Consider Image, Clientele, and Business Aims Relative to Your Restaurant's Location

One important set of questions involved in choosing a location revolves around the image you wish your restaurant to project. Since money spent on space is a fixed cost, one that you have to pay every month no matter how sales are, this is no trivial matter.

- How do you want your target markets to perceive your restaurant?

- Is there a "restaurant alley" or "fast food row" where your restaurant should be located?

But we suspect Cowboy Bob's location wasn't too shabby either!

Our restaurateurs clearly indicated to us that the amount of traffic, the site's visibility, and accessibility were all either very important or extremely important. In fact, not a single respondent stated that any of the three was "not important!" That's a pretty strong message.

When selecting a restaurant site, rate the following characteristics in terms of importance.

	"1"	"2"	"3"	"4"	"5"	Avg.
Amount of traffic	0.0%	1.2%	23.8%	33.3%	41.7%	4.2
Visibility	0.0%	0.0%	20.2%	38.1%	41.7%	4.2
Accessibility	0.0%	0.0%	17.6%	47.1%	35.3%	4.2
Lease/purchase terms	1.2%	1.2%	31.0%	31.0%	35.7%	4.0
Size	1.2%	11.9%	53.6%	25.0%	8.3%	3.3
Safety or security	2.4%	17.9%	45.2%	26.2%	8.3%	3.2

"1" = Not Important
"2" = Slightly Important
"3" = Important
"4" = Very Important
"5" = Extremely Important

We decided to force our restaurateurs to determine what single characteristic was the most important in determining location. We asked the following question:

"Of the six items listed above, which is the single most important aspect for site selection?"

Their responses:

31.3%	Amount of traffic
25.3%	Lease/Purchase terms
21.7%	Visibility
16.9%	Accessibility
4.8%	Size
0.0%	Safety/Security

Keep these responses in mind as you start to look at appropriate sites for your restaurant.

- Will you depend on walk-in business?

- Is the location consistent with the image you want to project? A fast food restaurant in a luxury location or a fine dining restaurant in a down-scale area is discordant.

- Where have your competitors set up shop? Why did they choose their location?

- What does your trade association offer to help in site selection?

- Check with your advisors (SCORE, SBDC, etc.). What do they recommend?

- What is the rent versus advertising cost trade-off? Low rent and high advertising costs tend to go together—and never work as well as the right site would have.

Location is a major choice and a critical choice. Take your time. For now, just look around and ask questions. You can make your choice later.

Chapter Three Action Plan

A. Concept Development (Type of Restaurant, Theme, Decor, Type of Service, etc.)

Action/Strategy	Target Date	Person Responsible	Results/ Comments
1. Refine your mission statement.			
2. Continue to research and narrow down the type of restaurant you will open.			
3. Continue your market research and determine the market and target markets you intend to serve.			
4. Begin to define the levels of service you will offer. Will you offer table-service, take-out service, a drive-thru window, delivery, or some combination?			
5. What are the ways you can differentiate your restaurant from the competition?			
6. Buy a copy of *The Restaurant Planning Guide*.			
7. Begin writing the concept portion of your business plan.			
8. Make a list of your competitors and identify their strengths and weaknesses.			
9. Identify and meet with realtors who deal with the type of property you will need.			
10. Start a list of important site criteria.			
11. Begin looking for sites that meet your criteria.			
12. Get traffic counts for the sites you are considering.			
13. Interview potential customers.			
14. Interview competitors or non-competitive restaurateurs.			

Action Plan, continued

B. Financial Issues (Pro Forma Income Statements, Cash Flow Statements, Balance Sheets, etc.)

Action/Strategy	Target Date	Person Responsible	Results/ Comments
1. Begin writing the financial portion of your business plan.			
2. Refine your financial statements to reflect more accurate figures from your research.			
3. Set up preliminary meetings with bankers.			
4. Get your preliminary financial statements set up on a spreadsheet so you can play "what if" scenarios.			
5. Start to compare your numbers with industry averages from the National Restaurant Association.			
Add your own actions/strategies here.			

Action Plan, continued

C. Operational Issues (Menu, Kitchen Design, Work Flow, Patron Flow, etc.)

Action/Strategy	Target Date	Person Responsible	Results/ Comments
1. Interview potential customers.			
2. Begin to identify menu items and develop appropriate standardized recipes.			
3. Begin writing the operational portion of your business plan.			
4. Begin to think about the prices in the marketplace and the prices you will charge.			
5. Visit similar restaurants.			
6. Contact several contractors for rough estimates about renovations, equipment installation, and time schedules.			
Add your own actions/strategies here.			

Action Plan, continued

D. Legal Issues (Legal Entity, Permits and Licenses, State and Federal Income and Personal Taxes, etc.)

Action/Strategy	Target Date	Person Responsible	Results/ Comments
1. Meet with government personnel responsible for issuing liquor permits. Be certain that you can develop the necessary information in time for the appropriate government agency to process your application before your scheduled opening.			
2. Meet with government personnel responsible for issuing health permits. Be certain that you can develop the necessary information in time for the appropriate government agency to process your application before your scheduled opening.			
3. Set up preliminary meetings with insurance agents.			
4. Set up preliminary meetings with lawyers.			
5. Set up preliminary meetings with accountants.			
6. Get advice about the advantages and disadvantages of the various business entity forms.			
Add your own actions/strategies here.			

Action Plan, continued

E. Personal Issues

Action/Strategy	Target Date	Person Responsible	Results/ Comments
1. Develop a personal mission statement.			
2. Prepare your personal financial statements.			
3. Prepare your personal resume.			
4. Start writing the personal section of your business plan.			
5. Join trade associations, general business associations, and other appropriate professional groups.			
6. Continue to update your general management and restaurant management skills.			
7. Continue to update your computer skills.			
8. Continue to discuss your plans and their impact on your life with your family.			
Add your own actions/strategies here.			

FOUR

Six to Four Months Before Start-Up

SIX MONTHS TO FOUR MONTHS BEFORE OPENING, concentrate on making the picture developed over the past six months more precise. This helps you set the stage for numbers and dollars to enter the picture. Avoid the fun-with-numbers approach wherein the financial goals are set first, then the vision and assumptions warped to fit those goals. If the financial model you will build in Chapter Five is to be useful to you, it must flow from your vision and assumptions.

This time period is the most critical in the planning process. Decisions you make now will impact your restaurant well into the future. Be certain your decisions are well thought through and are based on good, solid information.

You can now begin to address several substantive problems. Among these are determining the type of restaurant, naming your restaurant, choosing the location and deciding who your professional advisors will be. Once you know what your restaurant will be, and who your lawyer, accountant, and banker will most likely be, you can get answers to a still more specific set of questions, such as whether or not to incorporate, what bookkeeping and accounting systems make sense, and what key skills and information your business will still need.

Whatever type of restaurant you decide to open, remember there are several important components for any restaurant—often referred to as the value equation.

Value = Ambiance + Food + Price + Service

You need to continually address these items throughout the planning stages. We asked our restaurateurs, "What one, single item do you consider the most important component of the value equation?" They responded as follows:

5.1%	Ambiance
52.6%	Food
9.0%	Price
33.3%	Service

One of the respondents commented, "Good food, friendly service, clean facilities—you can't miss!" Another indicated. "The quality of food and service go hand-in-hand. If you don't have both you will not be successful."

Need we say more?

Decide on the Type
of Restaurant You Will Open

If you haven't already done so, now is the time to determine the type of restaurant you will open. There are too many differences among the types of restaurants to put it off any longer. Not only will the financial projections you have to make at this time be greatly impacted by the type of restaurant, but so will location, staffing needs, advertising, construction and renovation, equipment, furniture and fixtures, and just about every other aspect of your restaurant.

Will your restaurant be full service (with waiters and waitresses) or limited service (fast food)? If full service, what type of guests will it cater to? Families and casual dining (with a relatively low average check) or fine dining (with a higher average check)? Will you serve liquor? If limited service,

Pot Belly Deli Cafe
Brighton Park Shopping Center
Frankfort, NY 40601
Est. 1995
502-696-8494

My husband Ken and I dreamed and planned for two years about our restaurant. We felt we were pretty well financed and mentally prepared for what might jump up and bite us in the first two years. We were mistaken. We had a tremendous amount of luck that helped us in the beginning and we learned fast but what we envisioned was not reality. We are happy with the progress we've made and see ourselves as a success even though we certainly aren't getting rich. Our advice to others would be:

• The financing wasn't anywhere near what we required (figure out what you need, then double or triple it).

• Comparison shop until you drop for EVERYTHING.

• Buy used every time if you can.

• Work in a restaurant similar to the one you want before you do it yourself.

• Have a strong and understanding support group in business and personal relationships.

• Don't move to a different part of the country to start your business unless there is no other way.

We opened a deli cafe that serves freshly prepared pasta, green salads (12 to 15 a day), superior meat and cheese sandwiches, all with a twist. We also serve homemade soup and chili, which was widely advertised. On our first day open, a customer came in and after gazing at the menu board for several minutes asked: "Do you have fried catfish?" I answered "No sir." He asked, "Do you have coleslaw or cornbread?" I again answered "No Sir." He then turned to leave and as he was walking out the door his final comment was, "You know, if you don't serve fish and cornbread you're never goin' make it in this town."

Well, he was wrong.

Akhila Klein

will there be seating? Will there be a drive-through window (if not, you had better reconsider your decision)? What meals will you serve? These—and many more questions—will have to be answered once you decide on the type of restaurant you will operate.

Make certain your decision is being made on the research you conducted in Chapter Two and Chapter Three. Your market research, your analysis of the competition, your analysis of trends, and your research into the voids in the marketplace should be the basis for your decision. Don't make your decision on what you like to cook or you like to eat. You may be the only person in that market segment.

You also need to consider the hours of operation, the days of the week, and the impact on your family and personal life that will also be determined by the type of restaurant you open. If your analysis and research indicates that the need is for a type of restaurant that will adversely affect your family and personal life—or is a type of restaurant that you're not interested in—now is the proper time to stop. Close this book, throw it in the garbage, and start to investigate entrepreneurial activities in another industry. Better to stop now than to continue with a venture that is doomed to failure. Remember, at this point in time your investment has primarily been one of time. From now on, your financial investment is going to begin and grow rapidly. (If all you learn from reading this book is that you shouldn't go into the restaurant business, then we feel that the money you paid for this book was well spent.)

As you design your menu, it's important to keep track of other things besides just the name of the menu items.

The restaurateurs in our survey ranked the importance of consistency far above any of the other attributes we asked them about. That should tell you two things. First, your customer will come to expect a certain type of food at your restaurant. If you continually radically change the menu they won't know what to expect and won't return. Second, the food had better be prepared the same way time after time. If you haven't started a recipe file yet, start to do so. If you don't have standardized recipes, start to develop them and include them in your operational plans.

In terms of the menu, rate the following in importance to your guests.

	"1"	"2"	"3"	"4"	"5"	Avg.
Consistency	0.0%	1.2%	5.9%	28.2%	64.7%	4.6
Menu prices	0.0%	5.9%	38.8%	43.5%	11.8%	3.6
Portion sizes	0.0%	7.1%	43.5%	42.4%	7.1%	3.5
Creativity	2.4%	12.9%	48.2%	23.5%	12.9%	3.3
Uniqueness	1.2%	25.9%	38.8%	22.4%	11.8%	3.2
Nutritional/healthy aspects	12.9%	36.5%	35.3%	10.6%	4.7%	2.6

"1" = Not Important
"2" = Slightly Important
"3" = Important
"4" = Very Important
"5" = Extremely Important

We also forced our respondents to select the single most important item. Our question was: "Of the six items listed above about food, what one is the most important to your guests?"

Their responses:

78.3%	Consistency
8.4%	Price
4.8%	Creativity
3.6%	Uniqueness
3.6%	Nutritional/Health aspects
1.2%	Portion size

Have you started your standardized recipes yet?

We also asked the restaurateurs in our survey who should design the menu. We asked, "Before opening, who should design the menu?"

They responded:

58.8% Chef and owner working together	
18.8%	Management team
12.9%	Chef as owner
11.8%	Owner
3.5%	General manager
1.2%	Chef

Respondents were allowed to reply to more than one option, thus the total is more than 100 percent. However, the implication is clear—unless you're both the owner and chef, make sure you're actively involved in planning the menu. Don't just tell the chef to do it and accept whatever he or she puts together. Remember, you're the one who has been doing all the research for the past six months, and your knowledge is important.

Decide on Your Menu

Now is the time to decide on your menu. Let us repeat that statement with a bit more emphasis: **Now is the time to decide on your menu! NOW IS THE TIME TO DECIDE ON YOUR MENU!**

We assume you get the picture. Unfortunately, too many potential restaurateurs get ready to open the door and then think about what they will serve. It's too late! There's too much depending on what the menu is to let it go to the last minute.

The items you will be serving will impact many things in your restaurant: 1) the amount of refrigerated, freezer, and dry goods storage you will need; 2) the cooking equipment and other heavy equipment needs; 3) your china, glassware, and silverware needs; 4) the size of your staff, the skill levels of your staff, and the number of hours the staff will be required to work; 5) the type of decor appropriate for both the building exterior and the dining area; 6) and last but not least, the pricing structure and, therefore, the expected profit margins from each menu item.

Don't make the mistake of assuming you can adapt an existing kitchen facility to produce any menu you design. It doesn't work that way. Design a menu that is a result of your market research and then design the kitchen to produce those food items as effectively and efficiently as possible.

Name Your Restaurant

Naming your restaurant is a pleasant task. It makes it easier to visualize the business, and somehow makes the entire start-up process feel more real.

It is also an important task. The name you choose will position your restaurant in people's minds, affect the image you project, and have a major impact on your success. Some guidelines may help you think through the naming process. These are not intended to prevent you from being creative or whimsical but they are intended to help you avoid the unintended consequences of a hastily chosen name.

Naming a business is an important marketing decision. Keep in mind that one major marketing rule is to minimize customer (and prospect) discontent.

- *Keep the name straightforward and descriptive.* The name you pick should tell your markets what your restaurant is about, not baffle them. "Joe's" may or may not be a restaurant. "Joe's Italian Restaurant" leaves no doubt.

- *Make the name distinctive (if possible).* You still want to stand out from the crowd. "Jimmy's Harborside Seafood Restaurant" is clear and direct.

- *Avoid humor.* What you think is funny your markets may not. Humor is a dangerous marketing tool at best.

- *Shun grandiose descriptors.* "Supreme," "Universal," "Federal," and so forth have been overworked to the point where they are meaningless. Keep this in mind also when you write menu descriptions.

- *Don't pick the first name that comes to you.* Make a list. Ask your friends. Check the yellow pages, not just in your area but in other places. (If in doubt, don't use a famous name. Ask your lawyer.)

- *Try your business name out on some people who don't know you and your business idea.* They may give you positive feedback—or constructive criticism. Run it by your ad agency or marketing advisors. It's easy to change the name now. It won't be once you develop a logo, stationery, business cards, signs and put your phone number in the yellow pages.

Select Your Location

You've thought about where your restaurant should be located—now it's time to make your selection. Four months before opening should be enough time to arrange for all the improvements and changes you want to make, yet not too long a time to pay rent before making money. This also assumes you will be buying or

Determining the type of restaurant will obviously mean focusing on the menu and types of food you intend to serve, but don't forget about the service aspects which, as our survey showed, ranked second to food in the value equation. We asked our restaurateurs to rank some of the attributes of service and they provided the following responses.

In terms of service, please rate the importance to your guests of each of the following items.

	"1"	"2"	"3"	"4"	"5"	Avg.
Friendliness	0.0%	0.0%	18.8%	30.6%	50.6%	4.3
Attentiveness	0.0%	0.0%	23.5%	28.2%	48.2%	4.2
Guest recognition	1.2%	6.0%	11.9%	34.5%	46.4%	4.2
Timeliness	0.0%	0.0%	18.8%	51.8%	29.4%	4.1
Product Knowledge	0.0%	8.2%	22.4%	38.8%	30.6%	3.9

"1" = Not Important
"2" = Slightly Important
"3" = Important
"4" = Very Important
"5" = Extremely Important

It's interesting to note how high all these attributes were rated. Remember them when you get to Chapters Seven and Eight and when it's time to start hiring.

Again, we forced our restaurateurs to select the single most important attribute by asking the question, "Of the five service items listed above, what one is most important to your guests?" They responded:

39.3%	Attentiveness
31.0%	Friendliness
16.7%	Guest Recognition
9.5%	Timeliness
3.6%	Product Knowledge

leasing an existing building. If you plan to build a new structure go back to Chapter Two.

Check with your lawyer for zoning and licensing requirements. These will vary from one location to another, and an error can be extremely costly. Arrange to tour the facility with a representative of the health department. Now's the time to learn of potential problems.

Rent = Space Cost + Advertising

As a rule, it is safer to spend more on location and less on advertising than vice versa. Advertising always carries an element of risk. Choose your location based on your target markets' buying habits, patterns, and expectations. And remember what our survey respondents said in Chapter Three.

You will pay a premium for some locations—but if you try another one, the savings won't make up for the wrong location. Ever notice how certain kinds of businesses such as fast food restaurants, auto dealers, department stores and jewelry stores flock together? There's a good reason for it. If you know where the car dealers are, you can shop around. Competition increases everyone's business. An isolated fast food restaurant (or dealership or jewelry store) will slowly but surely fade. Few restaurants succeed as destination sites. Make sure that you are convenient and easily accessible to your guests.

Realize that Cheapest Is Not Always Least Expensive

Space cost is a combination of rent or mortgage payment, utilities, leasehold improvements, general spiffing up, security, insurance, and all related costs of having a place to conduct your business. A premium rent may be less expensive once you add up the bills than an apparently less expensive rental.

Choosing a location because the rent is cheap is risky. Your location speaks loudly to your customers, and if it says the wrong things you will lose sales. Your choice of location, like your choice of a business name, is mighty hard to change once you've committed yourself to it. Choose carefully, with your customers' and prospects' needs and habits in mind, and choose wisely. After all, it's more important for your customers to approve of your location than for you to approve of it.

Check with Your Local Health Department

Now that you have decided on the type of restaurant, the menu, and the location of your restaurant, make a trip to your local department of health. The professionals there should be considered a valuable resource—not the enemy—and now is a good time to start getting their advice.

Is the location you have selected zoned for a restaurant? Are there any problems with water, sewer, trash disposal, or other utilities? Does the existing kitchen—or the kitchen you intend to install—meet health codes, or will changes and modifications have to be made? Does the equipment already installed—or equipment you intend to install—have the appropriate designation, e.g., NSF (National Sanitation Foundation), and is it of the proper design? (Sinks, for example, should have rounded corners to make cleaning easier and to prevent the build up of food and dirt which harbor bacterial growth.) Will your employees be required to have certification in proper food handling techniques? The health department can help you answer these and lots of other questions.

Remember, you have both a moral as well as a legal responsibility to serve wholesome food. Proper food handling techniques and sanitation are critical and now is the time to get feedback from the health department so you can get started on the right foot—and avoid costly changes later.

Set Up a Network

Now that you've had time to research the organizations which might be useful, join them. As owner of a local start-up business, you should join your chamber of commerce and local restaurant association and be an active member. This is an important part of your marketing effort. The benefits outweigh the costs. You will find that as a new member with a new business you will receive a lot of business (and publicity) that otherwise would not have come your way. Local service organizations are another way to make lots of contacts in a short period of time.

Select Outside Advisors

The correlation between using outside advisors and success in business is so high that only the most hell-bent-for-failure individualists try to go it alone. "Using" means asking for advice and following it. Soliciting advice from experts and then not following it is silly.

There are two important kinds of advisors to try to recruit. The first includes your professional advisors. The second includes informal advisors, other business owners and friends. Running a business is a notoriously lonely affair, so recruiting this second group is important. Usually all you have to do is ask them for help and keep them informed. Professional advisors, on the other hand, have to be paid one way or another.

Choose and meet with your:

• Lawyer

• Certified public accountant

- Bookkeeping service

- Insurance agent

- Banker

- Advertising agent

- SCORE, SBDC, and other SBA counselors

- Consultants

You need a competent lawyer, accountant, insurance agent, and banker. Shop around for these professionals. Pick the ones you are most comfortable with. You'll have plenty to do without attempting to be your own lawyer and accountant (and anyway, only fools have themselves for clients).

If your start-up is going to be relatively simple, check out franchised bookkeeping services such as General Business Service or Comprehensive Accounting Corporation. They provide an excellent low-cost tax and financial advisory service for thousands of small business owners. As with any franchise, you have to pick and choose. Some franchisees will be more competent than others. The better ones can be strong resources for you as you move toward start-up. Make sure that your choice is willing to put your financial records in the format recommended in the *Uniform System of Accounts for Restaurants*.

If your restaurant involves complicated record keeping, talk to your accountant. He or she will set up (and even maintain) a bookkeeping system that's appropriate for your business.

You don't have the same level of need for an advertising agency. However, the cost of poor advertising and promotions is extravagant. Putting out the wrong message and creating the wrong image for your restaurant costs immediate dollars, but the opportunity cost of lost sales is tremendous. Once your advertising and marketing efforts are fairly routine you can economize (though if you have capable advisors you won't want to) but to make sure that you start out on the right foot, hire experts. Don't try to learn advertising and promotion techniques on the job.

Consultants (including the free or low-cost ones already mentioned) serve a variety of functions. The most important come from their depth of experience. They can save you time, money, and misspent effort. For example, a marketing consultant with 10 years' experience in the restaurant industry will have put together scores of marketing plans, monitored their progress, and made constant improvements. That experience, put to use for your start-up, can make all the difference. True, consultants cost a lot on a per diem basis. But you are buying their training and experience, not just their current time. If you can afford to invest in a marketing consultant at the outset, it's a wise move. Otherwise, talk with SCORE, SBDC, and SBA personnel and try to find the person with the best feeling for your business and its marketing problems.

How do you go about finding the right outside advisors?

• Ask other business owners.

• Call the professionals and ask for an appointment (a free consultation is often their best marketing ploy). Ask them for references and then follow up.

• Ask about their failures as well as their successes. Their responses will be revealing.

• How comfortable do you feel with them? The relationship with a professional doesn't have to be chummy, but you should feel confident in their discretion, integrity, and concern for your business.

• If you already have a good relationship with a banker, ask him or her for recommendations. Many banks keep a referral list of professionals which they share with customers.

• Ask other professionals. Your family lawyer can refer you to a business lawyer, for example.

Choose Your Restaurant's Legal Form

The legal form of your restaurant is an important choice, and in order to make it correctly you should rely on professional advice. Since the tax code is tens of thousands of pages long, and the penalties for making the wrong decision are so high, don't try to make this choice unaided.

While you can buy books on how to incorporate for pennies, you'd just waste your money. Put your recently selected lawyer and accountant to work helping you with this decision.

• Most small businesses are **sole proprietorships** (also known as "DBAs" for "John Jones 'doing business as' Four Corners Convenience Store," etc.). This is the simplest legal form, but there are some tax disadvantages to DBAs.

• **Partnerships** are more complex legally. Ask your accountant why so many professional partnerships have become corporations recently: "Smith & Jones, P.A." (professional association).

• **Corporations** have many flavors (for example, Subchapter S Corporations), some decided tax advantages, and much higher initial legal costs.

• **Limited Liability Corporations** (LLCs). Most states now have provisions for LLCs which combine some of the benefits of corporations with the benefits of partnerships. Check with your legal and tax advisors.

The right choice for your business depends on what your business will be doing, what its future is, and what your plans are. Once more: Don't make this decision yourself. Ask your lawyer and accountant for advice—and follow it.

Set Up Bookkeeping, Accounting, and Office Systems

The first step toward getting the operating information you will need to run your restaurant is to make sure that you have the right kind of bookkeeping system. Make sure you use the *Uniform System of Accounts for Restaurants*, which makes comparisons with other restaurants much more direct.

While you will need your accountant's assistance to set up your bookkeeping and accounting systems, semi-customized systems may be available through your trade association. These will save you considerable time and money, as they make it unnecessary for you and your accountant to reinvent standard practices.

Choose Your Bookkeeping and Accounting Systems (with Accountant)

You have a wide range of choices in your bookkeeping and accounting systems. Some are low-cost, but demand a lot of your time. Most small business owners don't want to spend a lot of time being the bookkeeper and prefer to hire someone to come in part-time. Others prefer to use patented "one-write" systems. Computerized systems are increasingly popular, and their cost is plummeting.

This is another choice that calls for professional advice. You want your systems to provide accurate, timely information in a format that will help you better manage your business. You don't have to become a CPA, but you should have enough familiarity with standard financial accounting practices to be able to read and use a balance sheet, an income statement, and a cash flow budget. (There is more on these in Chapter Five.)

- *Customized systems.* Designed for your business by a CPA (Certified Public Accountant), these double-entry systems (credits and debits) make it easy to spot errors. Some economic historians claim that the invention of double-entry bookkeeping was as important as the invention of the printing press to modern business. Don't worry about becoming an expert bookkeeper. Hire one instead, and your accountant will help you understand and interpret the results.

- *One-write systems.* For some businesses, one-write systems are ideal. These are also called "pegboard systems" because they use a pegboard to hold checks and invoices. You fill out the check or the invoice, a carbon copy of the pertinent information is recorded, and keeping accurate accounting records is greatly simplified.

General Business Service, for example, has a proprietary one-write system that is as simple to keep up to date as a checkbook. Your local business supply store may have other systems.

- *Computerized systems.* There are computerized one-write systems including one called, aptly enough, "One-Write Plus" (ordering information is provided in the Resources section) and computerized accrual systems. Ask your accountant which one would make the most sense for your business. As computers become more widespread, these programs have gone down in price and are now easier to use.

It is so important that you get timely and accurate financial information that computerized accounting systems alone justify purchasing an up-to-date microcomputer. With the revolution in both hardware and software, you can generate statements as often as you please, inexpensively, quickly and effortlessly. But make sure to have a qualified professional set up your computerized books, and train your bookkeeper.

All bookkeeping systems require careful, accurate data entry. Your accountant or business advisor can help you set up the books (decide what information to record and how to record it). But someone has to accurately make those daily entries and make the summary accounting reports that convert the data into useful information.

You may find that a bookkeeping service is ideal. Check around. Ask other similar businesses how they handle their bookkeeping and accounting and whether they are satisfied.

Accurate, timely information is so important in running a business that trying to economize in this area is like trying to economize on water when your house is on fire. Get the best assistance you can afford. It'll be worth it. To paraphrase Peter Drucker, if you have to ask why you need an accountant, you aren't ready to go into business, and if you can't afford a good accountant, you don't have enough money to go into business.

Get Business Forms for Interviewing, Personnel Records, and So On

Recent legal decisions have made keeping proper personnel records almost as important as keeping proper tax and accounting records. At this time, set up your personnel records, including application and interview forms.

Check with your SBDC or other consultants; they will know of local sources. If you can get application forms from large businesses (usually simply by asking), do so. They spend thousands of dollars to make sure they comply with the latest legal wrinkles. Best of all, take a course in basic personnel procedures.

- Why is this so important?

There are questions you cannot legally ask on an application or in an interview.

Some restaurant owners think "I know people" means having real personnel skills. Not the case.

Interviewing is a tough skill to learn. It's easy to be blinded by our own preconceptions. Structured interviews are one way to minimize bias.

Record keeping is another matter. You will need to keep records for tax and legal reasons, and it's far cheaper to do so correctly from the beginning than to reconstruct records at a later time. Ask your advisors for help. Ask a business professor who teaches personnel management for help.

Get a Taxpayer Identification Number

You have to get a taxpayer identification number for your business. The form is available from the IRS and can be filled out in minutes. Get it ahead of time because you'll frequently be asked for it.

Determine Your Office Equipment Needs

How do you determine what office equipment you need? Ask people already in business. Don't rely on office supply salesmen to give you unbiased advice. The less you have to spend the better, but there will be some items you cannot do without. By making some of these decisions now, four months before opening, you can scout out bargains and save some cash.

Take Business Courses

There are so many business courses that your problem may be where to start. In no special order, look into the following:

1. **Financial management courses.** These put bookkeeping and accounting information to work for you. You have to know how to read a balance sheet, a profit and loss (income statement), and cash flow budget. Ignoring financial management is a quick way to stunt your future.

2. **Marketing courses.** These include sales training, advertising, and other marketing skills. Marketing (the process of creating customers) is what business is all about. You can never learn too much about how to attract and retain customers.

3. **Personnel courses.** Hiring, managing, evaluating, and even firing personnel will probably be a constant challenge for you. Find out what the basic practices are. No need to reinvent them.

4. **Planning courses.** The SCORE pre-business workshops are a good example.

One of the great pleasures of owning a business is that it requires constant learning. Success comes from a host of incremental improvements: do this better, do that better ... You don't have to master everything. You do have to know enough to spot management omissions.

Take an IRS Tax Seminar

The Internal Revenue Service puts on short, useful seminars for new or prospective small business owners. They are worth the time and travel. These courses cover basic tax and record keeping requirements and take some of the fear out of dealing with the IRS.

Put Together an Outside Advisory Board

Although most small business owners don't have a board of directors, most could benefit from an advisory board's objective oversight and advice. Successful business owners go to great lengths to get such boards together, and then heed the advice given.

Where would you find advisors? Ask those persons you think could help you. They'll be flattered. The worst thing that could happen is that they'll say no. Talk to several of the following:

• Business friends

• Former employers or supervisors

• Retired business people from your industry

• Professionals

• Business professors

• Investors

• Consultants

• Experts in your field

Even one outside advisor will be invaluable. You will benefit from their experience and contacts; they benefit from involvement with a growing business. Even a personal friend who can intelligently listen to you makes a good sounding board. Business success comes from common sense and diligence. Outside advisors will help you preserve both.

Seek Out and Use Demographic Information

This is the Age of Information, right? What does that mean? First, computers and surveys and census reports and studies abound. Second, those who use that information will prosper, while people who ignore it or don't take the time to use it won't. Third, information is inexpensive power. And it's not that hard to access.

Demographic information about your market includes such factors as its age, gender, education and income level, location, buying habits, and hundreds of other descriptors. You can use this information to identify prospective customers, develop menu items and service levels to meet their demands and tastes, and make sound marketing choices.

For example, if you find that the population in your marketing area is becoming younger and more affluent, this information will influence your marketing decisions—and might compel you to replace your plans for a downscale cafeteria.

The amount of available demographic information is staggering. Ask your librarian for economic census information: you can find out how many people have bought refrigerators in selected zip code areas. Talk to your ad agency, too. Some other sources of help in securing and interpreting demographic information include:

- *Small Business Institute (SBI) programs*. Marketing professors who run SBI programs love demographic studies. They are intellectually stimulating, profitable to the business owner, and a great way for students to understand how important customers are to small business.

- *Regional and local planning commissions*. If you are fortunate enough to have a planning commission nearby, one of their skills is understanding demographic changes. Who is moving in? What kinds of economic changes is the area undergoing? What do they mean? Planning commissions are another one of those resources often overlooked.

- *Utility companies* often provide careful analyses of demographic changes which can help you make better decisions. Call their Office of Public Information for more information.

- *Real estate companies and bankers*.

- *American Demographics* magazine is a great resource for understanding what demographics can do for your business. Another good one is *Sales & Marketing* magazine. Check your library.

Chapter Four Action Plan

A. Concept Development (Type of Restaurant, Theme, Decor, Type of Service, etc.)

Action/Strategy	Target Date	Person Responsible	Results/ Comments
1. Decide on the type of restaurant you will open.			
2. Decide on the type of service you will offer. Table-service, counter service, take-out service, drive-thru window, combination?			
3. Determine how you will create value for your guests.			
4. Ask outsiders if they think your concept and ideas will create value for guests.			
5. Select your location.			
6. Check with the zoning board to ensure there are no problems with your intended usage at that location.			
7. Check with the local health department about your plans for that site.			
8. Check with the planning commission about site and building usage.			
9. Contact a contractor to develop a remodeling schedule.			
Add your own actions/strategies here.			

Action Plan, continued

B. Financial Issues (Pro Forma Income Statements, Cash Flow Statements, Balance Sheets, etc.)

Action/Strategy	Target Date	Person Responsible	Results/ Comments
1. Evaluate direct and indirect costs of various locations.			
2. Estimate remodeling and construction costs. Do they make sense in terms of your financial projections?			
3. Review your financial projections with your accountant.			
4. Review your financial projections with your banker.			
5. Review your financial projections with prospective partners or equity investors.			
Add your own actions/strategies here.			

Action Plan, continued

C. Operational Issues (Menu, Kitchen Design, Work Flow, Patron Flow, etc.)

Action/Strategy	Target Date	Person Responsible	Results/ Comments
1. Decide on your menu.			
2. Design the dining area, kitchen area, and lounge area.			
3. Determine your kitchen equipment needs and kitchen layout needs.			
4. Determine your office equipment needs.			
5. Determine your dining area equipment needs.			
6. Determine china, linen, and glassware needs.			
7. Set up your bookkeeping, accounting, and office systems.			
8. Buy a copy of *The Uniform System of Accounts for Restaurants* if you have not already done so.			
9. Determine the hours of operation for your restaurant.			
10. Start to develop control procedures and cash handling procedures.			
11. Start to test recipes and develop standardized recipes.			
12. Buy a copy of *The Restaurant Planning Guide* if you have not already done so.			
Add your own actions/strategies here.			

Action Plan, continued

D. Legal Issues (Legal Entity, Permits and Licenses, State and Federal Income and Personal Taxes, etc.)

Action/Strategy	Target Date	Person Responsible	Results/ Comments
1. Make a list of possible names for your restaurant.			
2. Review the list with outside advisors.			
3. Have the list reviewed to see what names are available and what names are already taken.			
4. Select a lawyer.			
5. Review site lease or purchase terms with lawyer.			
6. Select and register your business name.			
7. Consult with your lawyer about the best way to organize the business entity.			
8. Choose your restaurant's legal form.			
9. File the necessary papers to establish your restaurant's legal form.			
10. Get a taxpayer ID number (both state and Federal).			
11. Select an accountant.			
12. Get forms for a food service permit from the local health department.			
13. Get forms for a liquor service permit from the appropriate state agency.			
14. Select an insurance agent.			
Add your own actions/strategies here.			

Action Plan, continued

E. Personal Issues

Action/Strategy	Target Date	Person Responsible	Results/ Comments
1. Set up a network.			
2. Select outside advisors.			
3. Have an organizational meeting of your outside advisory board.			
4. Take business courses.			
5. Take restaurant management courses.			
6. Join the chamber of commerce.			
7. Join the state and local chapters of the National Restaurant Association.			
8. Join the local restaurant association.			
9. Talk with your family about how things are progressing. Get their advice and counsel.			
Add your own actions/strategies here.			

More: Six to Four Months Before Start-Up— Financial Projections

IF YOU KNOW WHAT QUESTIONS TO ASK, finding the answers is easy. Your financial statements will spit out a lot of answers about your restaurant if you use professional advice in setting up your books, take steps to ensure that the information you receive is timely and accurate, and use your financial statements to help you make decisions. Trying to take shortcuts is folly. Unless you are a trained CPA (and even in this case I'd have serious reservations), invest as carefully in your information system as you do in employees and equipment. Your information system will help you make the best use of these resources.

Determine Your Cash Needs

Strangely enough, financial analysis is the easiest part of your start up planning. You have to put your business ideas into standardized formats, which have evolved over centuries to make information easy to analyze, compare, and use. You may be unfamiliar with financial statements. But you are familiar with the kinds of questions they can be used to answer. For example:

- How much cash do I need to start my restaurant?

- Is this going to be a good investment?

- Can I make payroll every week?

- Will I make money?

- How much is my restaurant worth?

- How does my restaurant stack up against other restaurants?

- How many "bowls of soup" must I sell to break even?

- Can I afford to buy this machine, hire that person, borrow more money, enter a new market?

- At what point will I be too deep in debt?

Your financial statements will help you answer all of these questions and more. You don't have to be a financial wizard to gain these benefits, since financial accounting is rather straightforward. The more technical aspects can be handled by your accountant or other financial advisors (such as SCORE or SBDC counselors), but the numbers have to be based on *your* ideas.

This is particularly true during the start-up period, when the margin for error is very small. Once your business is up and running, your ideas will be corrected by experience. But now, the most you can hope for is to provide educated guesses based on your ideas, your research, and industry figures such as those provided by the National Restaurant Association. Table 5.1 provides average operating statistics. These industry figures will serve as your model. But you must use the *Uniform System of Accounts for Restaurants* in order to make any comparisons meaningful.

At a minimum, become familiar with the balance sheet (see Chapter Six) and the cash flow projection (also known as a cash budget) dealt with later in this chapter. These will help you answer the most pressing financial questions start ups face. The Profit and Loss Statement (also called an Income Statement) is useful too, but for start-up businesses the key question is: "Do we have enough cash to meet our bills?" The answer to that comes from the cash flow. The question "Am I making a profit?" is secondary, because it doesn't matter whether or not you are making a profit if you can't pay your bills. Break-even analysis helps quantify the sales levels you must reach based on your projected expenses and is used to decide how much a proposed addition (a new piece of equipment, a new employee, higher rent and so forth) will really cost you. Ask your accountant or other financial advisors for help on break-even analysis, as it depends on some tricky judgments about expenses.

All of these financial tools are important: Financial control, using the cash flow as a budget to hold down spending and the balance sheet to show the shifting balance between assets and liabilities, will spell the difference between making money and going broke.

The restaurateurs in our survey weren't shy about telling us the importance of realistic projections. We asked them, "Unrealistic projections often result in failure. Which factor is most important in developing realistic projections?" They responded (more than one response was permitted, thus the total is more than 100 percent):

49.9%	Accuracy of expense projections
33.7%	Accuracy of sales projections
19.3%	Accuracy of market analysis (demand)
9.6%	Other

Some of the comments they made included: "plan to work under the worst case scenario"; "always project the lowest possible sales and the highest possible expenses"; "start with expense projections on one-half your sales and see if it still works," etc. Their message is the same as ours—estimate expenses high and sales low. It's better to be surprised when your sales are higher than projected and your expenses are lower than projected rather than being surprised the other way.

We also asked for their comments on cash flow projections versus income statement (profit and loss) projections. More than two-thirds voted for cash flow.

"Which is more important:"

| 68.7% | Accurate cash flow projections |
| 31.3% | Accurate income statement projections |

Be certain you read carefully the section on projecting cash flow later in this chapter.

Table 5.1: National Restaurant Association* Operating Statistics

| | Full Service Average Check | | Limited Service | |
	<$10	>$10	Fast Food	Cafeteria
Income				
Food sales	86.2	77.2	97.5	98.7
Beverage sales	13.8	22.8	2.5	1.3
Total	100.0	100.0	100.0	100.0
Expenses+				
Cost of food sold	29.0	26.8	31.1	31.2
Cost of beverages sold	3.5	6.3	0.7	0.5
Salaries and wages	29.6	28.1	26.3	28.8
Employee benefits	4.8	4.6	2.5	5.3
Direct operating expenses	6.3	7.1	5.4	2.8
Music and entertainment	0.3	0.7	0.1	0.0
Marketing	2.8	2.8	4.9	4.3
Utilities	3.1	2.7	2.8	4.6
Occupancy costs	5.7	5.7	6.6	5.2
Repairs and maintenance	1.8	2.1	1.6	1.9
Depreciation	2.5	2.1	2.0	1.2
Other operating expense (income)	-0.4	-0.1	0.0	0.4
General and administrative	3.3	4.3	3.8	5.5
Corporate overhead	2.1	2.0	2.2	1.0
Interest	0.6	0.6	0.6	0.1
Other	0.3	0.5	0.4	0.0
Total	95.3	96.3	91.0	92.8
Income Before Income Taxes	4.7	3.7	9.0	7.2

+All expenses are expressed as a percentage of total sales.
* Source: http://www.restaurant.org/research/ratios.html

Review Preliminary Financial Objectives

Even if you have altruistic motives for starting your business, you still must make a profit to remain in business over the long haul. If you've come this far in your preparations for start up, you must have good reasons to think your business will be profitable.

Set Sales Objectives

By this point, you've had plenty of time (and reasons) to alter your original sales objectives. One of the main reasons for getting as familiar as you can with your industry and questioning people experienced in your field is to avoid the dangers of setting unrealistic sales objectives. Table 5.2 on p. 72, will help you forecast sales more precisely. For now, general answers to these questions are needed:

1. *What range of sales do you think you'll attain during the first year?* This should be based on your research. An answer such as "Between zero and $5,000,000" won't be much help. An answer such as "$350,000 to $500,000" will.

   Dollar Sales = Number of Units Sold x Price. In the restaurant business, the number of units sold is usually referred to as "covers." Thus, the owner of a 40 seat restaurant that serves 60 lunches will say he or she did 60 covers for lunch. (The term "turns" is also often used to describe volume. In this example, the restaurant owner would say he or she did 1.5 turns for lunch, meaning each seat was occupied 1.5 times—60 customers divided by 40 seats.) The term "average check" is used to describe the price. If the total sales for lunch were $195.00 in this example, then the average check for lunch would be $3.25 ($195.00 divided by 60 guests). Use the concept of covers and average check to help you estimate your sales. Estimate how many people you think you can or will serve in a day and multiple that figure by your estimated average check in order to get your estimated average daily sales. It's an easy matter to convert the daily average into a weekly, monthly, or annual estimate.

2. *What sales range do you want to hit in a few years?* This can be very general, since it is used as a long-range target only.

Set Profit Objectives

The same thinking applies to profitability. Check industry figures, talk with owners of businesses like yours, and ask your banker and other financial advisors for a reality check. While they will be less optimistic than you, listen to them.

Decide on Your Pricing Strategies

Pricing is a widely misunderstood strategic tool. Lack of courage in pricing may be the biggest single marketing error small-business owners make. There is a widely held perception that price drives all purchasing decisions, so in order to gain market share you have to slash prices below the competition. Wrong! This is the worst strategy possible. You cannot afford to be the cut-rate king.

Price and perceived value work together. Price is important. But it is not the only reason people buy things.

Look at it this way. Do you buy everything on price? Medical care? Cars? Food? Education for your children? You will find the matrix in Figure 5.1, p. 70 helpful in thinking through your pricing strategies.

Locate your restaurant and your competitors' restaurants on the matrix on p. 70. You might also want to consider other factors besides quality, for instance convenience, ambiance, service or exclusivity (snob appeal). All of these influence price and perceived value.

The traditional method of pricing menu items is based upon "food cost" (or food cost percentage), which refers to the cost of the raw food ingredients expressed as a percentage of the selling price and is computed by the following formula:

Computation of "Q"

"Q" refers to the "Quotient" or the cost of all other food items served with an entree. For example, a starch, a vegetable, a tossed salad, and bread and butter are included with the entree at no additional cost when ordering an entree, then the cost of food includes not only the cost of the entree, but the "Q" factor as well.

Assume the restaurateur's costs are as follows:

Baked Potato*	$0.10
or	
French Fries*	$0.40
or	
Onion Rings	$0.48
and	
Vegetable	$0.10
and	
Tossed Salad	$0.44
and	
Bread and Butter	$0.45
Highest Total	**$1.47**

* Only one of these three is included with an entree and the most expensive has been used to calculate the "Q."

Food Cost (Food Cost Percentage) =
(Cost of Raw Food Ingredients ÷ Selling Price) x 100

EXAMPLE

Assume the cost of all the ingredients needed to make a single portion of one of your entrees is $2.35. In addition, the "Q" (see sidebar) for a meal is $1.47, so the total cost for an order is $3.82. If the item sells for $9.95, the "Food Cost" of the item is:

Food Cost (Food Cost Percentage)

= (Cost of Raw Food Ingredients ÷ Selling Price) x 100

= ($3.82 ÷ $9.95) x 100

= .384 x 100

= 38.4%

Restaurants traditionally determine their desired food cost percentage and compute a selling price based upon the cost of raw food ingredients and the desired food cost percentage. Dividing the cost of raw food ingredients by the desired food cost percentage provides the suggested selling price. In the case of this example, the suggested selling price of the menu item, based on a desired 40 percent food cost, is $9.55, which was computed as follows:

Suggested Selling Price =

Cost of Raw Food Ingredients ÷ Desired Food Cost Percentage =

$3.82 ÷ 0.40 = $9.55

Thus, the restaurant should sell the item for $9.55 per portion if it wants to obtain a 40 percent food cost. In fact, the restaurant sells the item for $9.95, which results in a food cost of 38.4 percent. The reason for increasing the price was to compensate for the amount of labor required to prepare the item and the fact that the owner felt the market would perceive a greater value in the product and would pay a slightly higher price.

Figure 5.1: Price Matrix

Pricing is a major marketing concern. Price, quality, service and profitability are tied together in a complex web. While there are some mechanical formulas for cranking out price decisions, there are a few common sense guidelines that will help you develop a price range to work within.

a. Price = Product + Service + Image + Expenses + Profit. The menu prices you set should reflect not only the cost of food itself but also an intangible image factor. In an ideal situation, you would know how your customers and prospects perceive the value of what you sell and price accordingly. You also have to cover other expenses and profits.

b. Determine your pricing objectives. Identify your objectives. Are you trying to buy market share with low prices? (It won't work but you can always try!) Maximize profits? Remain competitive? Build up a new product line? Your general marketing objectives apply here. Pricing is inherently strategic, so be clear on your objectives.

c. Establish price ranges. This is defensive. Make sure that you charge enough to cover your costs. A break-even analysis (see *The Restaurant Planning Guide*) will help you establish the low end of your price range.

You have to cover your fixed costs with enough margin to survive, and this can be calculated in terms of both unit sales and dollars, thus helping you establish minimum prices.

At the high end, build your desired profit levels into the break-even equation and compare the prices you arrive at (on an item-by-item basis) to your sense of what the market will bear. Your customers won't pay more for your goods and services than they have to, and their perception of the value of your goods and services makes a very effective upper price limit.

d. Choose a flexible pricing approach. The four basic pricing approaches are full-cost pricing (which reflects your costs), flexible markups, gross margin pricing (which takes operating costs and marketing factors into account) and suggested or going rate. The last of these is the least desirable; it involves an endless game of follow-the-leader and ignores your cost structures. All of these approaches have their merits, however, and it makes sense for you to follow the one that makes the most sense for you.

For a fuller description of these pricing approaches, check with your accountant. A review of your pricing strategy is a valuable addition to planning, and should be part of your periodic financial and accounting reviews.

Avoid Competing on Price Alone

A good pricing strategy starts with costs and service level, then adds in elements of image (or positioning), and includes a profit component.

Some alternatives to price competition:

- Personalize
- Specialize
- Quality
- Service
- Value
- Convenience
- Safety
- Guarantees and warranties
- Attractive financing options
- Cleanliness
- Delivery

Don't make the mistake of underpricing in order to get customers. It doesn't work.

Forecast Sales

This is usually seen as the single most difficult part of financial projections. In many ways it is. Projecting sales is more art than science, and at best will be an imprecise affair. Too many outside factors affect sales level: economic conditions, competition, changes in consumer and business buying patterns, even the weather. But you still have to estimate the level of sales your business will strive to reach.

Express your sales forecasts in dollars, keeping in mind that the number of meals sold (i.e., "covers") times average check equals total sales.

Number of Meals Sold x Average Check = Total Sales

You will use the sales forecast in both the projected profit and loss statement (P&L) and in your cash flow projection.

Use a Three-Column Approach

The most effective and easiest way to project sales is to use a worst case/best case/most likely case scenario. For a start-up restaurant, this is even more difficult than for a going restaurant, since you don't have historical figures to guide your projections.

Break your anticipated sales down into small chunks. For example, look at a typical week and estimate the number of customers you will serve at each meal period. Then multiply the number of covers for that meal period by the average check for that meal period. Total your estimated dollar sales for each meal period to get an estimate for one week. A form similar to Table 5.2 is useful. After estimating the gross sales figures in the worst case and best case scenarios, choose an in-between figure for most likely. Add up the total of the most likely column and spread it over the 12 months of the cash flow projection worksheet on pp. 76–77.

It is important to remember that these figures are educated guesses at best. As your business progresses, your guesses will become more educated and

Table 5.2: Sales Forecast: For (month, year) to (month, year)

Sales	Low	Most Likely	High
Food			
Draft Beer			
Bottled Beer			
Liquor			
Wine			
Nonalcoholic Beverages			
Total Sales:			

more accurate. If you err, try to err on the conservative side. If you estimate sales lower than they turn out to be, you'll be far better off than pitching your estimate too high. Why? Because many expenses are geared to the sales forecast, and it is always easier to spend more than to save or cut back.

Also, make sure your estimates are reasonable. We knew one restaurateur who estimated serving 200 dinners each night. Since the restaurant only had 30 seats, we were skeptical of the estimated sales figure!

Get Assistance

Your accountant and other financial advisors will have had experience with businesses like yours, though, and should be called on to help you make reasonable guesstimates. Ask for trade figures. Robert Morris Associates' *Annual Statement Studies* is favored by bankers, but you will find better start-up financial ratios are available from trade associations, other people in your line of business, and perhaps from your accountant.

Trade association publications (ask the editor) sometimes run articles on how to forecast sales. If you can locate one of these, use it. What has worked for other people will work for you. Once you've been in business for a spell, you can safely try your own methods, but not now when you're beginning!

Many SBA, SBDC and SCORE counselors have had forecasting experience. So have some bankers and consultants. Ask them. If they haven't done much forecasting, they won't be much help. Good forecasting takes experience.

Determine Your Employee Needs

Before trying to work out a P&L projection, carefully look at your sales forecast. It will help you figure out how many employees you should have when you start up. Since personnel is the largest expense after cost of food sold, you don't want to add anyone to your payroll without a strong business reason.

Don't try to guess what your payroll expense will be and don't just pick the industry average. Averages are just that, average, and you certainly don't want to open an average restaurant. Your payroll cost is too critical to not do a thorough job of analyzing your expected payroll costs. Remember, we already discussed the impact that levels of service and the menu will have on your personnel needs. Therefore, take the time to calculate—as accurately as possible—what you should expect your payroll cost to be.

As you did when you estimated sales, break your anticipated payroll cost down into small chunks. The sample staffing schedule shown in Table 5.3 on p. 74 analyzes the staffing needs for a single day. The arrows show the starting time and ending time for each person. Each person's total hours worked

Table 5.3: Sample Staffing Schedule

Scheduled to Work (time columns: 9 10 11 12 1 2 3 4 5 6 7 8 9 10 11)

Position	Total Hours	Hourly Rate	Daily Pay
1st Cook	8	8.00	64.00
2nd Cook	8	6.50	52.00
Prep	6	5.50	33.00
Prep	8	5.50	44.00
Prep	5	5.50	27.50
Dishwasher	6	4.50	27.00
Dishwasher	8	4.50	36.00
Dishwasher	6	4.50	27.00
Bartender	8	4.50	36.00
Bartender	6	4.50	27.00
Hostess	8	5.00	40.00
Hostess	6	5.00	30.00
Hostess		5.00	0.00
Waitperson	8	4.25	34.00
Waitperson	8	4.25	34.00
Waitperson	5	4.25	29.75
Waitperson	7	4.25	29.75
Waitperson	7	4.25	29.75
Waitperson	7	4.25	29.75
Waitperson	7	4.25	29.75
Waitperson	7	4.25	29.75
Total	**139**		**$690.00**

Note: In addition to the above hourly employees, the kitchen manager/cook and the dining room manager are salaried employees at $400 and $350 per week respectively.

are then multiplied by the hourly rate to get the daily pay. Finally, the daily pay for all employees is totaled to get the total payroll cost for the day.

Start with a staffing estimate for the busiest day of the week and adjust accordingly for slower days. For example, on less busy days, perhaps only one bartender instead of two will be needed, one dishwasher instead of three, and three wait persons instead of five. However, remember, you will probably always need at least one bartender, one dishwasher, one wait person, and one cook.

Finally, don't forget to add those people who will work regardless of the volume. For example make a note of the kitchen manager and the dining room manager, both of whom are salaried. There may also be cleaning personnel, gardeners, and office workers to include.

Three questions you need to carefully consider:

• How many employees do you need?

• When should you hire them?

• Can you afford to hire full-time employees? Can you use part-time employees instead?

Project Your Cash Flow

The cash flow projection (or pro forma cash flow), which you will use as a cash flow budget, holds your feet to the fire of business realities. Your cash flow budget will help you hold down expenses and quickly spot problems. A business run without a budget lacks the discipline to survive, let alone prosper.

The nearest analogy to the cash flow budget is your checking account. You don't record deposits until you put cash in (corresponding to cash inflows). When you write a check you no longer have that money available (cash outflow, or cash disbursement). You record disbursements when the check is actually written, not before. All cash transactions, including checks, are recorded.

The key concepts for a cash flow projection are amount and timing. Disbursements and inflows are time-dependent. You have to exercise some discretion over when you incur expenses. Probably the most common error people make during the start-up period is to anticipate cash revenues sooner than they should. The general rule: Cash will come in more slowly and go out more rapidly than you expect.

Here's how to create your own cash flow projection. Fill in Figure 5.2, the cash flow projection forms on pp. 76–77. If some of the lines don't apply to your restaurant, or if you don't have the facts at hand yet, leave them blank. You can fill them in later. You want to make sure that cash inflows and outflows are shown in the months in which they fall. Remember: The keys to cash flow are amounts and timing.

Step One: Start with the easy part. Fixed monthly payments can be accurately figured. These include rent, salaries and benefits, insurance, equipment rental payments, and any monthly term-loan payment.

Step Two: Payments that aren't necessarily made monthly, but whose size and timing can be scheduled, come next. Ongoing advertising and marketing disbursements, some loan payments, and equipment purchases are examples.

Figure 5.2: Cash Flow Projection Form

	JAN	FEB	MAR	APR	MAY	JUN	JUL	AUG	SEPT	OCT	NOV	DEC	Totals
Cash Receipts													
Food Sales													
Beverage Sales													
Sales Receivables													
Other Income													
Total Cash Receipts													
Cash Disbursements													
Cost of Sales, Food													
Cost of Sales, Beverages													
Controllable Expenses													
Payroll													
Employee Benefits													
Direct Operating Exp.													
Advertising & Promotion													
Utilities													
Administrative & General													
Repairs & Maintenance													
Occupancy Costs													
Rent													
Property Taxes													
Other Taxes													
Property Insurance													
Interest													
Other Deductions													
Total Cash Disbursements:													

Figure 5.2: Cash Flow Projection Form, continued

	JAN	FEB	MAR	APR	MAY	JUN	JUL	AUG	SEPT	OCT	NOV	DEC	Totals
Cash Flow From Operations													
Cash Receipts													
Less: Cash Disbursements													
Net From Operations													
Cash on Hand													
Opening Balance													
Plus: New Loan (Debt)													
Plus: New Investment													
Plus: Sale of Fixed Assets													
Plus: Net From Operations													
Total Cash Available													
Less: Debt Reduction													
Less: New Fixed Assets													
Less: Dividends to Stockholders													
Less: Stock Redemption													
Less: Loans to Officers													
Total Cash Paid Out													
Cash Position—Ending Balance													

Step Three: Predictable payments are largely discretionary, though some are necessary but sporadic (licenses, for example). You have considerable choice over when to make most of these payments and will use these opportunities to juggle your cash flow.

Step Four: Now turn to the Cash Receipts. A separate section on projecting sales is given on p. 81. Using the "most likely" sales forecasts from there, try to spread out cash from sales and cash from receivables over the year. Most restaurant sales are for cash—or credit card sales which are treated the same as cash since you get the money as soon as you deposit the charge slip at the bank. The good news is that you don't have to wait for your money the way many other types of businesses do. The bad news is that—as in any cash business—there is a great deal of opportunity for theft. Therefore, it is critical that you set up systems to properly control cash and to be certain that all sales are properly recorded and all money properly received and accounted for.

Each month will probably be different, depending on the seasonality of your business. Seasonal patterns have such a dramatic effect on the shape of small business cash flows that you should seek out expert advice on the patterns your business will most likely face. (Debt, Investment, Sale of Fixed Assets, and Other will be treated in Steps Seven and Eight.)

Step Five: Variable payments depend on the level of sales. If sales are strong, you have to have inventories on hand to meet demand and may need extra help. Other variable costs will also increase. If sales are expected to be low, inventories can be low and other variable costs will shrink. Cost of goods sold will obviously vary with the volume of business.

Step Six: Turn to taxes. Ask your accountant for help. Taxes are part of the cost of doing business, and if you make money, you have to pay taxes. Their timing and amount vary—not at your whim but at the behest of the IRS. (You always have Uncle Sam for a partner, whether you want to or not.)

Step Seven: At this point, you can make the first cut at your cash flow. (It will change after you add back capital investment and proceeds from loans as outlined in the next two steps.) Figure the cash flow for each month: Net Cash Flow equals Total Cash Inflows minus Total Cash Outflows.

Step Eight: Figure Cumulative Cash Flow for the entire first year. If it continues steadily downhill, keep projecting until the cumulative cash flow definitely begins to turn up toward a positive figure. (If it never turns up, don't start the business unless your advisors can show you where your numbers have gone wrong.) For the first month, Cumulative Cash Flow equals Net Cash Flow. For the second month and beyond, add the new month's Net Cash Flow to the previous month's Cumulative Cash Flow to arrive at the new month's Cumulative Cash Flow.

You can now calculate how much capital your business needs (invested capital plus bank debt).

In Step Four, certain cash inflows were deliberately left to be treated later. The reason is that in all start ups there are negative cash flows from the beginning because revenues take a while to develop, while expenses start immediately. Inflows from new capital and loan proceeds cover these negative cash flows.

The Cumulative Cash Flow developed so far will typically show a pattern somewhat like this:

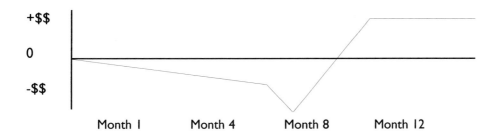

What causes this kind of pattern? Most start ups start out slowly, with some initial business coming in from being the new kid on the block. After a month or two, these sales dry up, and before sales start to increase again, significant sales and marketing efforts have to be put in place. Those are expensive (see Month 8) and usually lead sales by a month or more.

Assess Financial and Capital Needs

Step Nine: Look for the lowest cumulative cash flow in your projection. Multiply that figure by 150 percent (1.5) to arrive at the capital your business will need. Why multiply it? To be safe. Money won't come in as fast as you hope, and you can bet on it going out faster than you feel comfortable with. The timing and amount of Cash Inflows needed from New Capital and Proceeds of Loans can now be figured. The amount of cash from capital and loan proceeds should be spread out over the cash flow projection as needed. As a rule, capital comes in first. Then aim to borrow only as you must.

Meet with your banker for preliminary talks whether or not you will use bank credit. Your banker will help calculate your borrowing needs if you ask. Bring your cash flow statement and you will also establish your credibility in his or her eyes. But remember, bankers don't like to lend to restaurants, so be prepared to talk with other potential investors.

To minimize your costs, minimize borrowing. Use your cash flow projection to show your banker how much money you need, when you need it, how you will pay it back, and why it is a good investment of the bank's money.

Step Ten: Use the Cash Flow Budget.

It is appallingly easy to spend too much on equipment, or inventory, or interest, or new personnel. A budget, consulted before any purchase, helps keep spending down. You can always override it for compelling business reasons, but even then you would be wise to think twice.

The simplest way to use the budget is to set up a form at the beginning of the month that has your projected figures in one column and actual figures in the other. At the end of the month, compare the two columns. If disbursements are down, find out why. It's easy to miss a payment or reduce inventory without reordering. If disbursements are up, find out why. You may have prepaid a bill or overstocked. Then check inflows the same way. Look for variations; then seek the cause.

A Case Study

To help you understand the importance and usefulness of financial statements, consider the example of Giuseppe Pezzotti, a 35-year-old man who recently opened his own restaurant in a medium-sized Northeastern city.

Giuseppe was born and brought up in Italy. After graduating from high school, he worked as a waiter in a variety of restaurants in various European cities. He became an expert in service and his tables were frequently requested by restaurant patrons because of the exquisite service he provided.

At age 28, Giuseppe came to the United State to pursue his life-long dream of owning his own restaurant—and perhaps some day earn enough money to buy a Ferrari! However, he realized that he would need to gain more knowledge about the business of running a restaurant. In order to do so, Giuseppe did three things.

First, he gained experience about food preparation by working in the kitchens of several restaurants. These experiences helped him not only learn about food production—of which he had limited knowledge—but also helped him learn about ordering food, costing menu items, inventory control, portion control, scheduling, and many of the other managerial items that he had not been exposed to previously.

Secondly, he began to take general management courses at a local community college. Although it took him almost five years to do so, he eventually earned a business degree. The general management skills and financial management knowledge he learned complemented the restaurant knowledge he had gleaned from his years of working in restaurants.

Finally, he saved over $70,000 to help finance his first restaurant.

Giuseppe was finally ready to strike out on his own, and found a restaurant that was for sale by the current owner who was ready to retire. Although the restaurant was a traditional steakhouse, Giuseppe's market research showed that there was strong demand for an upscale restaurant featuring Northern Italian cuisine and the exquisite service that Giuseppe was capable of offering. His plan was to operate the dining room himself and hire an experienced chef to operate the kitchen.

The existing restaurant facility seated 50 people and was leased from the building's owner. Giuseppe negotiated a lease with a five year term at $24,000 per year. In addition, the adjoining store's lease was due to expire in 14 months and Giuseppe was able to include a clause in his lease that he would have the first option to lease the space if it became available. He figured he would be able to add 75 seats in the adjoining space if the restaurant was successful enough to warrant the expansion.

Since the existing decor was not conducive for Giuseppe's Northern Italian concept, he realized that he would have to redo the dining room and also make some changes to the existing kitchen in order to produce the menu he wanted to offer his guests. A contractor estimated the total costs of remodeling and purchasing and installing the additional equipment would be $100,000 and it would take two months to complete the renovations.

Giuseppe was able to purchase the tables, chairs, chinaware, silverware, and glassware from the existing restaurateur for $10,000 and was able to get the landlord to forgo the first month's rent since Giuseppe would be paying for the leasehold improvements.

Before signing the lease and committing to the project, Giuseppe put together a comprehensive business plan and showed the plan to several bankers, some of his college professors, and a number of restaurateurs he had previously worked for. Their comments and suggestions helped him modify and refine the written business plan.

Finally, he was able to conclude that the business had a reasonably good chance of success. He signed the lease, began the remodeling, and started on the thousands of other things that needed to be completed before the opening. He was on his way to his first Ferrari!

Giuseppe's Sales Forecast

Giuseppe had to use a number of assumptions in order to forecast what would be reasonable sales in his restaurant once it opened. His research led him to believe that it would be reasonable to average 50 meals per day (he intended to be open only for the evening dinner meal) and that he could reasonably expect to have an average check for food of $20 per guest and an average check for alcoholic beverages of $4 per guest.

He used these assumptions to project average daily sales of $1,000 per day for food (50 guests x $20 per guest = $1,000) and $200 per day for alcoholic beverages (50 guests x $4 per guest = $200).

Giuseppe used these daily sales to forecast weekly sales of $7,200 (he intended to be open six days per week) and annual sales of $360,000 (he intended to be open 50 weeks per year).

Case Figure 5.3 shows the calculations Giuseppe made to forecast the daily, weekly, and annual sales figures. Food sales include the sales of all food items and beverage items (e.g., coffee, tea, soft drinks). The cost of such beverage items is charged against food cost. Beverage sales include the sales of all beer, wine, liquor, and other alcoholic and nonalcoholic beverages whose cost is charged against beverage cost.

Giuseppe expected there would be very little variation in sales due to seasonality, which made his forecasting a bit easier. If your restaurant will be located in an area that experiences seasonal variations, then you may need to do several sales forecasts—one for each season you expect.

Giuseppe's Expense Forecast

Case Figure 5.3 also shows the expenses Giuseppe forecasted. While it is not possible to predict exactly each expense, the more effort expended in trying to get actual numbers, the more meaningful the projections will be. Giuseppe forecasted his expenditures in the following manner.

Cost of Food Sold. Giuseppe used a 36 percent cost of food sold. Although this is slightly higher that the national average, Giuseppe determined this percentage by developing standardized recipes and pricing out each menu item. For a detailed explanation of determining the cost of food sold see *The Restaurant Planning Guide*.

Cost of Beverages Sold. Giuseppe used a 30 percent cost of beverages sold to compute this expense.

Total Cost of Sales. This amount is determined by the sum of the cost of food sold and the cost of beverages sold.

Gross Profit. This amount is determined by subtracting the total cost of sales from the total sales ($1,200 per day – $420 per day = $780 per day).

Other Income. Giuseppe has not included any additional income. Use the *Uniform System of Accounts for Restaurants* for examples of what should be included in this figure.

Total Income. This figure is the amount of gross profit plus other income.

Case Figure 5.3: Giuseppe's Sales and Expense Forecast

	Daily	x 6 = Weekly	x 50 = Annually
Number of Seats	50		
Number of Meals per Day (Covers)	50	300	15,000
Average Check (Food)	$20.00		
Average Check (Beverage)	$4.00		
SALES			
Daily Food Sales			
(50 covers x $20.00/cover)	$1,000.00	$6,000.00	$300,000.00
Daily Beverage Sales			
(50 covers x $4.00/cover)	$200.00	$1,200.00	$60,000.00
Total Sales	**$1,200.00**	**$7,200.00**	**$360,000.00**
EXPENSES			
Cost of Sales			
Cost of Food Sold (36%)	$360.00	$2,160.00	$108,000.00
Cost of Beverages Sold (30%)	$60.00	$360.00	$18,000.00
Total Cost of Sales	**$420.00**	**$2,520.00**	**$126,000.00**
Gross Profit	$780.00	$4,680.00	$234,000.00
Other Income	$0.00	$0.00	$0.00
Total Income	**$780.00**	**$4,680.00**	**$234,000.00**
Controllable Expenses			
Payroll	$350.00	$2,100.00	$105,000.00
Employee Benefits	$17.50	$105.00	$5,250.00
Direct Operating Expenses	$84.00	$504.00	$25,200.00
Advertising and Promotion	$36.00	$216.00	$10,800.00
Utilities	$30.00	$180.00	$9,000.00
Administration and General	$48.00	$288.00	$14,400.00
Repairs and Maintenance	$24.00	$144.00	$7,200.00
Income Before Occupancy Costs	**$190.50**	**$1,143.0**	**$57,150.00**
Occupancy Costs			
Rent	$80.00	$480.00	$24,000.00
Property Taxes	$0.00	$0.00	$0.00
Other Taxes	$0.00	$0.00	$0.00
Property Insurance	$18.00	$108.00	$5,400.00
Total Occupancy Costs	**$98.00**	**$588.00**	**$29,400.00**
Income Before Int. and Deprec.	$92.50	$555.00	$27,750.00
Interest	$20.00	$120.00	$6,000.00
Depreciation	$48.00	$288.00	$14,400.00
Other Deductions	$0.00	$0.00	$0.00
Income Before Income Taxes	**$24.50**	**$147.00**	**$7,350.00**

Payroll. Giuseppe determined that he would need to draw a minimum of $24,000 per year from the business in order to support himself (of course, he hoped the business would be profitable and he would also get sizable profits to supplement his weekly draw). Since the restaurant would be open 300 days per year, this translated into $80.00 per day. Other salaries and wages included a chef at $39,000 per year ($130.00 per day), one dishwasher/prep person at $7.00 per hour for eight hours ($56.00 per day), and two waitstaff at $6.00 per hour for seven hours per day each ($84.00 per day total). Thus, the total daily payroll cost was estimated to be $350.00 per day ($80.00 + $130.00 + $56.00 + $84.00 = $350.00).

Employee Benefits. Giuseppe estimated this figure at five percent of payroll.

Direct Operating Expenses. This expense includes items that vary directly with the volume of business in the restaurant (e.g., paper supplies, dishwashing chemicals, chinaware, silverware, glassware, laundry, etc.). For a complete explanation of the items and categories see the *Uniform System of Accounts for Restaurants*. Giuseppe estimated this expense at 7 percent of sales.

Advertising and Promotion. Giuseppe estimated this at 3 percent of sales, just slightly higher than the national average.

Utilities. The local utility company provided Giuseppe with an estimate of $9,000 per year, which Giuseppe converted to $30.00 per day since the restaurant will be open 300 days per year.

Administrative and General. Estimated at 4 percent of sales, just slightly below the national average. For a complete explanation of the items and categories see the *Uniform System of Accounts for Restaurants*.

Repairs and Maintenance. Estimated at 2 percent of sales.

Income Before Occupancy Costs. Total income less all controllable expenses ($780.00 − $350.00 − $17.50 − $84.00 − $36.00 − $30.00 − $48.00 − $24.00 = $190.50).

Rent. Giuseppe's lease is $24,000 per year or $80.00 per day ($24,000 per year divided by 300 days per year open).

Property Taxes. Giuseppe's landlord is responsible for paying all property taxes.

Other Taxes. There are no other taxes that Giuseppe is responsible for.

Property Insurance. Giuseppe received an estimate of $5,400 per year from his insurance agent.

Total Occupancy Costs. This figure equals the sum of rent, property taxes, other taxes, and property insurance.

Income Before Interest and Depreciation. This amount equals the income before occupancy less rent, property taxes, other taxes, and property insurance.

Interest. Giuseppe borrowed $50,000 from the bank at 12 percent interest to pay for leasehold improvements. (The remaining $50,000 came from Giuseppe's savings.) The annual interest is calculated at $6,000.00 ($50,000 x .12 = $6,000) or $20.00 per day ($6,000 per year divided by 300 days per year that the restaurant is open = $20.00 per day).

Depreciation. The leasehold improvements ($100,000) will be depreciated over seven years for an annual depreciation expense of $14,285 ($100,000 divided by 7). Since the restaurant will be open 300 days per year, this calculated to $47.62 per day ($14,285 divided by 300 = $47.62). Giuseppe rounded this figure up to $48.00 per day.

Restaurant Profit. Profit equals the income before interest and depreciation less interest and depreciation ($92.50 – $20.00 – $48.00 = $24.50).

Giuseppe found it easier to estimate his expenses on a daily basis and then multiply by six to get a weekly figure and then multiply the weekly figure by 50 to get an annual figure. The annual figure shows that—if everything goes according to the estimates—the restaurant will have a pretax profit of $7,350. Since Giuseppe is the sole owner of the business, he can use this money to pay off some of his loan earlier, to buy additional assets for the restaurant, or to take out of the business for his own personal use—a downpayment on his Ferrari perhaps!

Giuseppe's Projected Profit and Loss

An Income Statement or Profit and Loss Statement shows all income when it was earned and all expenses when they were incurred. The combination of Giuseppe's sales forecast and expense forecast is an Income Statement for Giuseppe's Restaurant. Case Figure 5.4 on p. 86 shows Giuseppe's projected profit and loss, with the center column using the numbers that Giuseppe has projected. This column is labeled "expected," since these are his best estimates. The other two columns are labeled "10% Lower" and "10% Higher" and are used to provide some information if the estimates do not prove to be accurate.

Should all the revenues and expenses turn out as expected, the restaurant will make a profit of $7,350 in its first year. This is in addition to the $24,000 that Giuseppe will draw as salary which has been included in the payroll figure.

Should the restaurant not do the amount of sales that Giuseppe has estimated, then the profit will change accordingly. The column labeled "10%

Case Figure 5.4: Giuseppe's Projected Profit and Loss

	10% Lower	Expected	10% Higher
SALES			
Food Sales	$270,000.00	$300,000.00	$330,000.00
Beverage Sales	$54,000.00	$60,000.00	$66,000.00
Total Sales	**$324,000.00**	**$360,000.00**	**$396,000.00**
EXPENSES			
Cost of Sales			
Cost of Food Sold (36%)	$97,200.00	$108,000.00	$118,800.00
Cost of Beverages Sold (30%)	$16,200.00	$18,000.00	$19,800.00
Total Cost of Sales	**$113,400.00**	**$126,000.00**	**$138,600.00**
Gross Profit	$210,600.00	$234,000.00	$257,400.00
Other Income	$0.00	$0.00	$0.00
Total Income	**$210,600.00**	**$234,000.00**	**$257,400.00**
Controllable Expenses			
Payroll	$105,000.00	$105,000.00	$105,000.00
Employee Benefits	$5,250.00	$5,250.00	$5,250.00
Direct Operating Expenses	$22,680.00	$25,200.00	$27,720.00
Advertising and Promotion	$10,800.00	$10,800.00	$10,800.00
Utilities	$9,000.00	$9,000.00	$9,000.00
Administration and General	$14,400.00	$14,400.00	$14,400.00
Repairs and Maintenance	$7,200.00	$7,200.00	$7,200.00
Income Before Occupancy Costs	**$36,270.00**	**$57,150.00**	**$78,030.00**
Occupancy Costs			
Rent	$24,000.00	$24,000.00	$24,000.00
Property Taxes	$0.00	$0.00	$0.00
Other Taxes	$0.00	$0.00	$0.00
Property Insurance	$5,400.00	$5,400.00	$5,400.00
Total Occupancy Costs	**$29,400.00**	**$29,400.00**	**$29,400.00**
Income Before Int. and Deprec.	$6,870.00	$27,750.00	$48,630.00
Interest	$6,000.00	$6,000.00	$6,000.00
Depreciation	$14,400.00	$14,400.00	$14,400.00
Other Deductions	$0.00	$0.00	$0.00
Income Before Income Taxes	**($13,530.00)**	**$7,350.00**	**$28,230.00**

Lower" has food sales reduced to $270,000 and beverage sales lowered to $54,000. The cost of food sold and cost of beverages sold are reduced accordingly. All the controllable expenses—with the exception of direct operating expenses—remain the same, since they will not be reduce if fewer people walk in tonight. The direct operating expenses have been reduced since they vary as a percentage of sales. Occupancy costs, interest expense, and depreciation have not been reduced since they will not change if fewer customers come to the restaurant. The result of 10 percent lower sales is a loss of $13,530 dollars—not a pleasant thought to Giuseppe. However, the analysis is important to see the impact on the business of fewer customers so that contingency plans can be made before the fact rather than after.

Conversely, the third column labeled "10% Higher" shows the impact on more customers. Food sales and beverage sales have both been increased 10 percent in this scenario, as have cost of food sold and cost of beverage sold. The controllable expenses have remained the same since they will not be impacted by 10 percent more customers walking in tonight—the exception being direct operating expenses which vary directly with sales. Occupancy costs, interest expense, and depreciation also have not been changed since they remain fixed. The results of this scenario are, obviously, much more attractive since the profit jumps to $28,230—certainly enough to make the downpayment on the Ferrari!

Giuseppe's Cash Flow Projections

Cash flow statements show the sources of cash coming into the business and the flows of cash from the business. Such sources and uses of cash are determined when the money is received or when the money is spent. Giuseppe will need to predict two major periods of cash flow. The first is before the business actually opens, and the second is after the business has opened. Case Figure 5.5 on p. 88 summarizes these two projections.

Before the restaurant opens, Giuseppe will provide the business with $70,000 of his own money and $50,000 from a bank loan. He will use these funds to make the necessary leasehold improvements, buy tables, chairs, chinaware, etc., pay one month's rent, one month's advertising, one month's utilities, and one month's insurance. There will be a remaining cash balance of $5,900 when the business opens.

After opening, Giuseppe can expect cash sales of $30,000 per month (all sales are treated as cash since credit card sales are paid by the bank as soon as they are deposited) and cash expenses of $28,188, leaving a positive monthly cash flow of $1,813 ($21,750 annually). The major difference between the income statement expenses and the cash expenses is that

Case Figure 5.5: Giuseppe's Projected Cash Flow

	Before Opening	Monthly Operations	Annual Operations
Sources of Cash			
Personal Savings	$70,000	$0	$0
Bank Loan	$50,000	$0	$0
Food Sales	$0	$25,000	$300,000
Beverage Sales	$0	$5,000	$60,000
Total Sources	**$120,000**	**$30,000**	**$360,000**
Uses of Cash			
Leasehold Improvements	$100,000	$0	$0
Tables, chairs, chinaware etc.	$10,000	$0	$0
Operating Expenses			
Cost of Food Sold (36%)		$9,000	$108,000
Cost of Beverages Sold (30%)		$1,500	$18,000
Payroll		$8,750	$105,000
Employee Benefits		$438	$5,250
Direct Operating Expenses		$2,100	$25,200
Advertising and Promotion	$900	$900	$10,800
Utilities	$750	$750	$9,000
Administration and General		$1,200	$14,400
Repairs and Maintenance		$600	$7,200
Rent	$2,000	$2,000	$24,000
Property Insurance	$450	$450	$5,400
Interest		$500	$6,000
Total Uses	**$114,100**	**$28,188**	**$338,250**
Cash Flow (Sources – Uses)	**$5,900**	**$1,812**	**$21,750**

depreciation is not included on the cash flow statement since it is a non-cash expense. The cash flow statement does not show any amortization of the bank loan. The loan principal would also have to be paid and the monthly amount would be determined by the terms that Giuseppe arranged with the bank when he borrowed the money.

Conclusions from the Financial Forecasts

All-in-all, the restaurant shows promise. The Sales and Expense Forecast, the Projected Profit and Loss Statement, and the Projected Cash Flow all seem reasonable and attainable. Leasing the building—rather than constructing a new building or buying an existing building—significantly reduces the cash necessary to get into business and greatly improves the chances for success.

The projected financial statements provide support to the feasibility of the project as outlined in Giuseppe's business plan.

Chapter Five Action Plan

A. Concept Development (Type of Restaurant, Theme, Decor, Type of Service, etc.)

Action/Strategy	Target Date	Person Responsible	Results/ Comments
1. Gather industry operating statistics for the type of restaurant you are planning to open.			
2. Get contractors.			
Add your own actions/strategies here.			

Action Plan, continued

B. Financial Issues (Pro Forma Income Statements, Cash Flow Statements, Balance Sheets, etc.)

Action/Strategy	Target Date	Person Responsible	Results/ Comments
1. Determine your cash needs.			
2. Investigate options for obtaining the financing necessary to open.			
3. Review preliminary financial objectives.			
4. Compare your financial projections to industry averages.			
5. Project your cash flow.			
6. Review your cash flow analysis with your accountant.			
7. Review your financial projections with other restaurateurs.			
8. Review your financing needs and projected financial statements with your banker.			
Add your own actions/strategies here.			

Action Plan, continued

C. Operational Issues (Menu, Kitchen Design, Work Flow, Patron Flow, etc.)

Action/Strategy	Target Date	Person Responsible	Results/ Comments
1. Decide on your pricing strategies.			
2. Forecast sales.			
3. Determine your staffing needs.			
4. Research salary and wage levels.			
5. Cost out your menu items (determine the cost of goods sold for each item).			
6. Compute your "Q."			
Add your own actions/strategies here.			

Action Plan, continued

D. Legal Issues (Legal Entity, Permits and Licenses, State and Federal Income and Personal Taxes, etc.)

Action/Strategy	Target Date	Person Responsible	Results/ Comments
1. Gather the necessary financial information about your business you may need for your liquor license application.			
2. Gather the necessary personal financial information you may need for your liquor license application.			
Add your own actions/strategies here.			

Action Plan, continued

E. Personal Issues

Action/Strategy	Target Date	Person Responsible	Results/ Comments
1. Continue to improve your general business knowledge.			
2. Continue to improve your restaurant business knowledge.			
Add your own actions/strategies here.			

SIX

Four to Two Months Before Start-Up

BASIC MARKETING PLANS INCLUDE BENEFITS TO the customer, target marketing, and watchful concern for the competition. Reviewing the non-financial objectives and sales forecasts helps ensure that your latest thinking governs your projections. Securing financing and insurance coverage takes longer than many anticipate—two months is none too long a time to plan on. Financing will be dependent on your sales and cash flow assumptions, so they should be carefully annotated, even if no outside financing will be required. Your money is important too.

Prepare Your Marketing Plan

A marketing plan helps you figure out ways to find and keep customers, reach your sales goals, and keep your business efforts concentrated on those areas which have the best payoffs (both short- and long-term). It is built around your customers: their menu item and service preferences, their perception of your restaurant, and their changing interests.

This shouldn't be a major literary effort. Answer the questions—and keep asking and answering them as you go along.

Know your markets. Know your product/service and the benefits they offer. And know your competition. This is information at work.

Continue to pursue a sharper focus, acquiring a more detailed knowledge of the people who compose your target markets. You can never know your markets too well.

- At a minimum, answer these questions about your average prospect:

  ＊ How old?

  ＊ Male or female?

* What educational level?

* What income?

* What occupation?

* What dining preferences?

* What benefits do you provide—service, speed, convenience, atmosphere?

* What buying patterns?

* How can you profitably reach them (through which promotion and advertising avenues)?

* And, most important: How can you find more people like them?

Answer these questions, and keep asking them, or your competition will eat your dust. For some reason, very few restaurateurs are willing to ask and answer these questions on an ongoing basis. It takes work, but work makes winners. You can get help from trade publications, vendors, and most of all from your own observation and research. If you find that you aren't keeping up on this research, question your motivation for going into business. Markets are not static. They change. The owner who is prepared for these changes wins.

Make a Benefits List

You may think you sell a service or a product. Your customers buy benefits.

Features and benefits are closely related, but have to be kept separate. Features are used to describe what you sell: a service may be fast, relaxed, exquisite, available at unusual hours, delivered to your home or office. Your product (menu items) may be large, small, prepared differently, or difficult to get elsewhere. All of those are features. Benefits, on the other hand, describe why the customer is buying your product or service. He or she wants convenience, economy, and personalized attention.

Thinking of your restaurant, how would your customer answer the question: "Why should I go there?"

A benefits list helps you keep advertising costs down (ad agencies need to know what's in it for the customer), make product or service decisions (by keeping you focused on your market's desires, not your preferences), and beat the competition (they won't ordinarily be keeping the customers' preferences in mind). The basic idea is to make sure that you offer only what your market wants to buy.

Your research (both hot and cool) should have given you good ideas on what your markets want. Some ideas come from shopping competitors, some from questioning vendors, some from trade research. The big danger is to assume that you represent your markets' tastes so well that this research is not needed. That's the best way to stock up on buggy whips or Edsels or eight-track tape decks.

Is your research thorough and up-to-date?

Set Up Competitor Files

Your competition is just as smart and motivated as you are. Many of them are better established. Some will be better financed, have more experience, or have other advantages over you. What can you do to fight back?

Keep track of everything your nearest competitors do. Keep records of their ads, their promotions, their financial dealings. If they expand or open a second restaurant, you need to know. Competitor files are simply manila folders, one for each competitor, which you use to hold the information you gather.

Keep these files up-to-date and periodically review them, and you will know more about your competitors than they know about themselves. When do they run sales? What benefits do they stress? Are they going after new target markets, or trying to buy market share, or competing on quality? Are they consistent or scatter brained? How are their personnel: polite? haughty? well-trained? slovenly? Shop them. Call them and note how they answer the phone.

Know your competitors well enough so you know what they will do before they do.

Review Non-Financial Objectives: Image

Your business image will be developed by (among other factors) your markets, quality of food and service, price strategy, location, personnel, and advertising/promotion efforts.

Advertising/promotion includes stationery, business cards, signage, and public relations as well as ads and brochures. Many beginning business owners skimp on these apparently secondary areas, but it's an expensive economy. You only get one chance to make a first impression, and once that impression has been made it's hard (and costly) to change your image. If you intend to do catering—either on-premise or off-premise—these items and your promotional brochures and menus become even more critical.

- *Product/service and markets.* Test for a fit. Certain market segments want certain products or services. Menu selections, food quality, level of service, convenience, location and price are all important. So is consistency. Give it to them.

- *Location.* You chose your location with marketing uppermost in your thoughts. The leasehold improvements should continue along the same track. Will the premises be what your markets would expect and appreciate? The decor should be chosen to please them, not you.

- *Employees.* Hiring the right employees in the first place is simpler than hiring the wrong employees, then trying to remold them.

  * What kind of employees do your markets expect?

  * Who does the competition hire?

  * What is customary? (Unless you have extremely strong reasons to deviate from the norm, don't.)

  * What educational level is required?

  * How should employees dress?

  * How important is grooming and appearance to the function of the job? (Your answer to this question had better be: "Extremely!")

  * What training would help differentiate your employees from everyone else's?

  * Should your employees be local, or doesn't it matter?

  * Your employees represent your business to the public. Once again, place your markets' preferences and expectations ahead of your own. They're the ones who will pay the bills.

Review Sales Forecasts

As the start-up date approaches, go over your sales forecasts again. You may have gleaned some information that would cause you to change your original estimates, and when you sit down with your banker (or, more likely, your backers, including family or friends), you want to make sure your forecasts are conservative. If your sales forecasts have changed, your cash flow forecast (another name for your cash flow projection) will change too. Your updated thinking has to be reflected in your cash flow.

Prepare a Preliminary Balance Sheet

A well-prepared balance sheet is mandatory. Your banker needs it. You need it. Your accountant or bookkeeping service will need it. A balance sheet, like the cash flow, is a tool to help you better manage your business. The balance sheet is often compared to a snapshot bearing a date: it shows what your company looks like at a given moment (see Figure 6.1).

The balance sheet weighs what you own (assets) against what you owe (liabilities). The difference between the assets and the liabilities is net worth (owner's equity), sometimes used in figuring the value of the business.

Figure 6.1: The Balance Sheet

ASSETS	LIABILITIES
Current Assets	**Current Liabilities**
Cash	Taxes payable
Notes receivable	Salaries payable
Accounts receivable	Notes/loans payable
Inventory for sale	Accounts payable
Other inventory	Current portion long-term debt
Supplies	**Total Current Liabilities**
Prepaid expenses	
Total Current Assets	**LONG-TERM LIABILITIES**
	Notes
FIXED ASSETS	Term loans
Real estate	Mortgage
Fixtures and leasehold	Loans from officers
Improvements	**Total Long-Term Liabilities**
Equipment	**Total Liabilities**
Vehicles	
Goodwill	**NET WORTH**
Other	Subordinated debt
Total Fixed Assets	Retained earnings
	Invested capital
	TOTAL LIABILITIES
TOTAL ASSETS	**AND NET WORTH**

The format of the balance sheet is governed by a simple rule: assets and liabilities are both listed in order of their immediacy. Those assets that are nearest to cash are listed ahead of those assets that are used to maintain the business (the so-called fixed assets). Those liabilities that are nearest to being due are listed ahead of long-term debt, and all liabilities are listed ahead of the permanent capital (invested capital) and owner's equity, which won't turn to cash until and unless the business is sold.

A glossary containing definitions of the terms used in the balance sheet is provided on p. 180.

Filling in your balance sheet is easy once you know what all the terms mean. No mathematics more complex than addition and subtraction is involved. What you are trying to find out is how your business measures up against other businesses and how your assets and liabilities are distributed.

Depreciation and amortization are technicalities best left to your accountant. They affect asset values by writing their purchase and installation costs off as expenses over the expected life of the asset according to some rather arbitrary tax codes. Ask your accountant to help you.

Using the Balance Sheet

Balance sheets are designed to show how the assets, liabilities and net worth of a company are distributed at a given point in time. The format is standardized to facilitate analysis and comparison. Do not deviate from it.

Balance sheets for all companies, great and small, contain the same categories arranged in the same order. The difference is one of detail. Your balance sheet should be designed with your business information needs in mind. These will differ according to the size of your restaurant and the amount of information that your bookkeeping and accounting systems make available.

The categories can be defined more precisely. However, the order of the categories is important and you should follow it. They are arranged in order of decreasing liquidity (for assets) and decreasing immediacy (for liabilities). A brief description of each principal category follows:

1. **Current Assets:** cash, government securities, marketable securities, notes receivable (other than from officers or employees), accounts receivable, inventories, prepaid expenses, any other item that will or could be converted to cash in the normal course of business within one year.

2. **Fixed Assets:** land, buildings, equipment, leasehold improvements, other items that have an expected useful business life measured in years. Depreciation is applied to those fixed assets that, unlike land, will wear out. The fixed asset value of a depreciable item is shown as the net result of cost minus accumulated depreciation.

3. **Other Assets:** intangible assets such as goodwill, notes receivable from officers and employees, deferred charges such as pre-opening expenses, cost of liquor license, deposit on franchise or royalty contract.

4. **Current Liabilities:** accounts payable, notes payable, accrued expenses (wages, salaries, withholding tax, FICA), taxes payable, current portion of long-term debt, other obligations coming due within one year.

5. **Long-Term Liabilities:** mortgages, trust deeds, intermediate and long-term bank loans, equipment loans (all of these net of the current portion of long-term debt, which appears as a current liability).

6. **Net Worth:** owner's equity, retained earnings, other equity.

7. **Footnotes:** You should provide displays of any extraordinary item (for example, a schedule of payables). Contingent liabilities such as pending

lawsuits should be included in the footnotes. Changes of accounting practices would also be mentioned here.

If you need to provide more detail, do so—but remember to follow the standard format. If your balance sheet is assembled by an accountant, the accountant will specify whether it is done with or without audit. If you do it yourself, it is without audit. The decision to use a CPA (Certified Public Accountant) should be made carefully for tax and other legal reasons.

Some financing sources (banks or other investors) may want to see balance sheets projected for each quarter for the first year of operation and annually for the next two. This would quickly show changes in debt, net worth, and the general condition of the restaurant, and could be another helpful control document. You may wish to have a monthly balance sheet (easily done with a microcomputer-powered accounting system), but for many businesses, a year-end balance sheet is all that is required.

Preliminary Balance Sheet Analysis

1. **Working Capital**. Working capital is calculated by subtracting current liabilities from current assets. Cash is only a portion of working capital.

   A low or negative working capital position is a major danger signal. A firm with this working capital situation is said to be illiquid. Because owner's equity is less than the debt, the creditors in effect "own" the business, and bankers would be reluctant to extend further loans. Among possible solutions to this type of problem would be a working capital loan (long-term, to be repaid from operating profits), sale of fixed assets, or financing accounts payable by arranging to spread payment over a longer term. The best solution is to get a new equity investment.

2. **Comparison**. Comparison of year-end balance sheets over a period of years will highlight trends and spotlight weak areas. Compare your restaurant to other, similar operations by ratio analysis.

3. **Ratio Analysis**. This technique permits comparison in terms of percentages rather than dollars, thus making comparisons with other restaurants more accurate and informative. Among the more useful ratios are:

   A. *Current Ratio*. This measures the liquidity of the company, its ability to meet current obligations (those coming due during the current year). It is calculated by dividing current assets by current liabilities. However, you need to know exactly what is represented by the figures to make a meaningful analysis. Inventory composition, quality of receivables, time of year and position in the sales cycle are all possible factors affecting the current ratio.

   B. *Acid Test*. This is another measure of liquidity (sometimes called the Quick Ratio), and it is calculated by dividing the most liquid assets (cash, securities and possibly current accounts receivable) by current liabilities.

To get trade figures for your restaurant, try the following:

Although banks are notorious for not lending money to restaurants, many of the restaurateurs in our survey indicated that they were able to obtain financing from banks. We asked: "What were your major sources of financing for your first restaurant?" They responded (more than one answer permitted):

57.5%	Personal Savings
53.8%	Banks
26.3%	Family/Friends
15.0%	Private Investors
13.8%	Financial Partner
1.3%	Small Business Venture Funds

We were pleasantly surprised to learn that more than half had received at least some financing from banks. However, we strongly suspect that the restaurateurs were also contributing a substantial part of the financing themselves. To get a better understanding of the lender's perspective, we asked, "From a lender's perspective, which is the most important factor they consider for lending money to start a restaurant?" The responses:

39.3%	Owner's Previous Experience
28.6%	Loan to Equity Ratio
28.6%	Well Developed Business Plan
23.8%	Other
10.7%	Owner's Personal Connections

Not all respondents had received funding from banks. Some of the comments they made included: "banks only lend on secured assets, if you have none then forget banks!"; "banks hate restaurants and bars so it's a waste of time"; "personal liquid assets, banks don't lend to restaurants otherwise."

What should be clear is that, in order to have a chance of obtaining any financing from banks, you had better have some excellent previous experience in the restaurant industry, be willing and able to put up a good deal of the funds from your own personal sources, and have a well developed business plan (have you bought The Restaurant Planning Guide yet?).

- The National Restaurant Association and state and local restaurant associations.
- *Annual Statement Studies*, which your banker will usually have, available from the Robert Morris Associates.
- A friendly competitor, perhaps in a non-competing location.
- Your banker and accountant.

Secure the Necessary Financing

Most start up restaurants rely on house money (a shorthand term for savings, inheritances, investments from friends and relations, cash value of life insurance policies, and equity in a residence or other assets) to leverage more money out of a bank.

If you can avoid borrowing, by all means do so. But you will be a rare bird indeed. You may want to set up a bank loan anyway, to prepare for future growth needs. Bankers like to have credit experience with borrowers before lending substantial sums, so a small loan repaid on schedule can pave the way for obtaining greater sums in the future.

The assumption, however, is that you will go where all small businesses go sooner or later: to the banker to raise some cash.

Before you visit your banker, make sure that your balance sheet, sales forecast, and cash flow projection are updated and thoroughly documented. Credibility with your banker is a great asset, but one that is hard to gain and easily impaired. Since your balance sheet and cash flow have been prepared on the basis of your research and plans for your business, you have to be the person to talk with your banker. Bring along your financial advisor if you wish, but be prepared to answer most of the questions ("Why do you think this sales level will be reached? What if it isn't?") yourself.

You will find that you need either collateral or a co-signer. Banks like collateral because it shows that you are committed to the success of your business and won't walk away from it if things get rough. A co-signer can provide a depth of collateral that satisfies the important bankerly concern about the security of the loans they make (by law, banks have a fiduciary responsibility to their depositors which makes risky loans illegal). The Small Business Administration guarantees certain loans, which makes banks more willing to lend to start ups. If you need or would qualify for an SBA or other guarantee, your banker will tell you. A warning: SBA loans tend to tie up collateral, and can take much longer to process than the usual business loan. Seek out one of the SBA's preferred lenders, banks that can short cut the application process, if you have to rely on an SBA guarantee. You can get a list of preferred lenders from the SBA.

Use Your Cash Flow Forecast and Your Balance Sheet

This is where your cash flow projection and balance sheet are invaluable. There is no better way to demonstrate competence and commitment to your banker or other financing source than to present a clear, well-documented set of financial statements.

As noted above, the cash flow will show you the amount of capital that you need. If you have had the foresight to keep your banker involved from early on in the cash flow forecast process, this will be simple. If not, the cash flow will provide an excellent framework to discuss your real financing needs. The balance sheet will have to be revised after you secure financing, but that's a trivial task. At this stage, the balance sheet shows how the assets and liabilities stack up.

• How much debt should you take on?

• What kind of debt makes the most sense?

• What will your debt needs be in six months? In a year? Your long-term goals come into play when you discuss basic capitalization. Your banker can (and will) help you think through these needs.

If the response is that you are undercapitalized, get more capital. If you can't, don't start your business until you have adequate capital.

Bankers are conservative. They have to be. Their advice is based on working with many small businesses, and if you disagree with their advice they should be able to explain their position to your satisfaction. Remember that it is in your mutual interest to determine the most sensible debt structure for your business. If your banker suggests a different structure than you had planned on, listen to him or her. You will learn something that will ultimately help you, even if you wind up looking for another bank or banker.

Open Bank Accounts

Bankers are in business to make money by lending out their depositors' money. If you plan to use a bank's credit services (loans, credit cards and so on), offer them your deposit business while negotiating your loan or credit card. They can tell you what kind of deposit service makes sense for you, and as banking becomes increasingly competitive, will probably require that you bank with them if you borrow from them.

If You Will Accept Credit Cards, Make Arrangements Now

You may want to offer credit to your markets yourself, but credit is a profession that takes a lot of skill. Credit cards are a great way to shift the burden of passing credit judgments and collecting cash to organizations who know how. The cost will range from 1.5 to 7 percent depending on your business, your bank's experience, and the amounts involved. Most businesses find that the average sale is sufficiently higher when credit cards are used to warrant the bank's discount. Setting up a credit card account takes 30 to 60 days.

A Case Study, Continued

Giuseppe's Balance Sheet

Giuseppe's Opening Day Balance Sheet (see Case Figure 6.1) shows that the business has $128,000 worth of Assets and $128,000 of Liabilities and Net Worth. The numbers are based on the following information:

Current Assets. Current assets are assets with an expected life of less than one year.

Cash. This is the amount of cash that Giuseppe's restaurant has left after buying assets and paying expenses during the preopening period. The cash flow statement in part one of this case (Case Figure 5.5 on p. 88) shows what Giuseppe bought and paid for.

Food Inventory, Beverage Inventory, and Supplies Inventory. Giuseppe made arrangements with local purveyors to purchase food, beverages, and supplies and to pay them within 30 days. These numbers represent the cost of the inventory that Giuseppe has received at the restaurant.

Fixed Assets. Fixed assets are assets with an expected life of more than one year.

Case Figure 6.1: Giuseppe's Balance Sheet

Opening Day, 199X

ASSETS			LIABILITIES & NET WORTH		
			Current Liabilities		
			Accounts Payable	$8,000	
Current Assets			Total Current Liabilities		$8,000
Cash	$5,900				
Food Inventory	4,000		Long-Term Liabilities		
Beverage Inventory	3,000		Bank Loan	$50,000	
Supplies Inventory	1,000		Total Long-Term Liabilities		$50,000
Total Current Assets		$13,900			
			Total Liabilities		$58,000
Fixed Assets					
Leasehold Improvements	$100,000		Net Worth		
Furniture, chinaware, etc.	10,000		Giuseppe's Investment	$70,000	
Preopening expenses	4,100		Retained Earnings	0	
Total Fixed Assets		$114,100	Total Net Worth		$70,000
Total Assets		**$128,000**	**Total Liabilities & Net Worth**		**$128,000**

Leasehold Improvements. This represents the cost of the renovations and equipment that the contractor installed.

Furniture, Chinaware, etc. This is the cost of the tables, chairs, chinaware, silverware, and glassware that Giuseppe purchased.

Preopening Expenses. These are the expenses that Giuseppe had before opening for business. They were paid for and are shown on the cash flow statement in the first part of this case study.

Current Liabilities. Current liabilities show money owed that is expected to be paid within one year.

Accounts Payable. This is the amount the Giuseppe owes the local purveyors for the inventories they supplied him with but which he hasn't paid for.

Long-Term Liabilities. Long-term liabilities show money owed but which is not expected to be paid off for more than one year.

Bank Loan. This is the money received from the bank.

Net Worth. This represents the owner's claims to the business if all the assets were sold and all the liabilities paid.

Giuseppe's Investment. This is the amount of money that Giuseppe originally invested in the business.

Retained Earnings. Although zero now since the business has not started, this figure will represent any profits that the business makes and which Giuseppe decides to leave in the business rather than withdrawing as a dividend.

Total Liabilities and Net Worth. The total liabilities and net worth, $128,000, is the same as the total assets. Thus, the statement "balances."

Giuseppe's opening day balance sheet isn't as useful a tool as it will be in several months or a year. After being in business a while, his balance sheet will more closely resemble those of other restaurants. It is important, however, to keep the balance sheet straight from the start. It forms part of the tax record, helps measure progress, and provides a fixed point for comparison from year-to-year and with other businesses.

Chapter Six Action Plan

A. Concept Development (Type of Restaurant, Theme, Decor, Type of Service, etc.)

Action/Strategy	Target Date	Person Responsible	Results/ Comments
1. Refine your mission statement.			
2. Continue to update your competitor files.			
3. Continue to define and identify your target market.			
4. Make a list of the benefits you will offer your customers.			
5. Focus in on your restaurant's image, public relations efforts, and other promotional plans.			
6. Develop advertising plans.			
Add your own actions/strategies here.			

Action Plan, continued

B. Financial Issues (Pro Forma Income Statements, Cash Flow Statements, Balance Sheets, etc.)

Action/Strategy	Target Date	Person Responsible	Results/ Comments
1. Meet with your banker.			
2. Establish bank relationships and secure financing.			
3. Open bank accounts.			
4. Make arrangements for accepting credit cards.			
5. Review your financial objectives.			
6. Review sales forecasts.			
7. Review staffing levels and labor costs.			
8. Update your statement of cash flows.			
9. Prepare your preliminary balance sheet.			
Add your own actions/strategies here.			

Action Plan, continued

C. Operational Issues (Menu, Kitchen Design, Work Flow, Patron Flow, etc.)

Action/Strategy	Target Date	Person Responsible	Results/ Comments
1. Schedule leasehold improvements.			
2. Get bids and order tables, chairs, equipment, and other "big ticket" items.			
3. Meet with purveyors.			
4. Prepare written job descriptions.			
5. Determine a recruiting plan for hiring employees.			
Add your own actions/strategies here.			

Action Plan, continued

D. Legal Issues (Legal Entity, Permits and Licenses, State and Federal Income and Personal Taxes, etc.)

Action/Strategy	Target Date	Person Responsible	Results/ Comments
1. Meet with lawyer to review financing arrangements.			
2. File application for health department permit if you haven't already done so.			
3. File application for liquor license if you haven't already done so.			
4. Meet with insurance agent and apply for workers' comp and other required insurance policies.			
Add your own actions/strategies here.			

Action Plan, continued

E. Personal Issues

Action/Strategy	Target Date	Person Responsible	Results/ Comments
1. Continue to update your general management skills.			
2. Continue to update your restaurant management skills.			
Add your own actions/strategies here.			

SEVEN

Two Months Before Start-Up

TWO MONTHS AND COUNTING. TIME IS GETTING SHORT. By now you have made the decision to continue with your restaurant start-up. You have secured the necessary financing (or at least the commitments), have selected the location, have gotten estimates for any remodeling and renovations that need to be made, and have refined your financial projections to the point where they show a reasonably good chance of financial success (there's never any absolute guarantee that a restaurant start up will be successful).

If you haven't accomplished all these things, go back and do so—and push back the opening date until two months after they have been completed.

There are still a multitude of items to accomplish, and you will find that everything will become more and more hectic as opening day approaches. All the more reason for accomplishing as much as possible as soon as possible.

Secure Insurance Coverage

Select your business insurance agent with the same care you chose your lawyer, banker, and accountant. Since this area calls for professional-level expertise, think carefully whether your friendly life insurance agent has the skills to handle your business coverages.

Insurance is a necessity. You are legally required to provide certain coverages (for example, worker's compensation, unemployment). Your creditors will require other coverages. And prudent management calls for basic liability coverages.

- *Mandated coverage.* Social security (FICA) and worker's compensation are legally mandated. Depending on your location, other coverages may be required. Your insurance agent can lead you through the legal thicket. These are costs of doing business.

- *Life, Accident and Health Insurance.* Health care is a powerful employee benefit and recruiting tool. It is hideously expensive and rapidly increasing in cost, but until a more rational health care system is established, you're stuck with it. Employees can (and perhaps should) share the cost. Shop around. Trade associations and chambers of commerce sometimes offer better terms through group plans than a small business could secure alone. This is a hard area to make decisions about, so take your time.

  * What are the limits of the policies offered?

  * What is covered? What isn't?

  * If you cover the first $1,000 (or more) yourself, what happens to the premium?

  * Is coverage non-cancelable?

  * How about existing conditions?

  * How long is the waiting period before coverage begins?

At a minimum, speak to at least five different life, accident and health insurance providers.

- *Liability and other coverages.* As owner of a restaurant, make sure that you are protected against the normal expected business risks: fire, theft, accident, and so on. Your insurance agent will work out a package covering the basics; ask what other coverages might apply. Ask about liquor liability if you will be serving alcoholic beverages. It can be complicated—and expensive.

Answer Legal Questions

Check in with your lawyer again to make sure you are in compliance with zoning and local business ordinances. If you have to apply (or reapply) for a license or other legal requirement, two months is probably sufficient time. Liquor licenses may take longer.

Determine Image, Advertising, Promotion, and Public Relations Strategies

Put your customers first. How will they perceive your restaurant?

Sources of low-cost help in determining how best to represent your business include SCORE and SBDC counselors. You can also ask other business owners who they like; this is often the best way to locate capable local marketing help. Big ad agencies aren't interested in small budgets, but local agencies are often interested in locating clients to grow with. The smaller agencies (including public relations and marketing consultants) are usually the best bet for start-up businesses, although you will have to pay for their expertise.

As before, shop to find the right marketing help for you and your restaurant. The ideal case is where the expert becomes part of your management team, helps you save money by sparing you the expense of learning to do it yourself, and most important of all, helps ensure that your promotional efforts (advertising of all sorts, public relations, and any other promotional efforts including grand openings) are targeted to the right people through the right media for your business.

This presupposes that a lot of work on your part has already been done. You know who you want to reach, you know what their hot buttons are apt to be and what benefits you can offer them—and what you can afford to spend in your marketing efforts. A general word of caution: Make sure to budget enough money for two kinds of promotional activity. The first is the ongoing campaign to keep your name in front of your markets. This is usually going to be local media (newspaper, yellow pages, perhaps radio or cable TV). The second is for special events, opportunities, or challenges such as sudden intense competition.

Use Outside Experts

The dangers of do-it-yourself, or of using inexperienced folks, is that you put out the wrong message to the wrong people at the wrong time through the wrong media. If any one of these areas is bungled (message, market, timing, or media) you are throwing money away. Advertising that fails to achieve any positive goal is expensive no matter how little cash you spend on it. Talk to ad agencies and other experts. Use your advisors to corroborate your instincts or back up your decisions—but be prepared to pay for marketing and promotional skills. Once you know what you are doing you may be able to pull some of this effort back in-house, but for a start up, don't even think of cutting corners here. It won't work.

Check Logo and Name of Business Again

Once you have some promotional help, go over the name of your business, your logo, and other materials that help project your image to your public with the experts. Sometimes very subtle changes can make a big difference. You may not be tuned in to the effect of different typefaces, or colors, or the implications of a name, but these can be important. Even big companies have been known to blow this one. Chevrolet vigorously promoted their Nova model in Spanish speaking countries before discovering to their chagrin that "No va" means "doesn't go." Hardly an endorsement for a car.

Establish Promotion and Advertising Plans

Solicit help from your ad agent or other promotional experts on your grand opening strategy. New restaurants have an advantage (they are new) and a disadvantage (nobody knows about them). How you address opening promotions can make a substantial difference over the first several months of your business.

If you plan a celebration, line up the entertainment or the musicians or whatever now, well in advance of the opening. If you plan a media blitz, plan ahead.

You may be able to garner some publicity (business openings are news), but to make sure of the best timing and placement, give the editor a lead time of six weeks or so; trade publications usually require even more lead time, while local papers and stations need less. Ask your promoting specialist for advice on putting together press releases. It's an art that you can learn, but you don't want to waste the edge being new gives you.

Order Professionally Designed Printed Materials

The danger of sending out printed materials with the wrong image can be minimized by getting a graphic artist to design your stationery, invoices, business cards, invitations, and so on. The cost is minimal, the benefits long-lasting.

Contact Food and Beverage Vendors

You should start to contact the various food and beverage vendors you will be ordering from. Although food and beverage inventories represent a relatively small amount in comparison to large retail stores or manufacturing companies, you will need to determine the sources you will be using. Since many food products are highly perishable, you will need to get deliveries quite often. For other items (e.g., canned goods and paper supplies), you may be limited by storage space and the fact that you don't want to tie up a lot of money in inventories. Now is the time to make your initial contact with vendors. Some of the questions you should be asking are:

• What days of the week will you deliver to me?

• Is there a minimum order size for delivery?

• How much lead time do you need for orders?

• What are the payment terms?

• How do I set up an account?

• What is your policy on returned items at the time of delivery? At a later date?

You should also check with other restaurateurs to see if there is a local buying cooperative or other organization to help you take advantage of volume discounts.

Complete Improvements to Your Facility

Extensive remodeling, painting, carpeting, and so on takes time. The earlier you can pin down your contractor (or spring some of your own time if you plan to do it yourself) the better. Ideally, these jobs will be completed 30 to 60 days before opening to give you time to alter things that don't look or feel right and to make sure that those special lights you order actually arrive.

Some occasionally overlooked improvements include:

• Office walls

• Special lighting fixtures

• Heating/ventilating/air conditioning

• Display areas: shelving, carpeting, display windows

• Storage areas

• Point-of-purchase displays

• Security improvements: alarms, shutters, lights

Food service equipment dealers—and even your food and beverage vendors—can be a big help in the layout and design of your kitchen and dining areas. They may also help you by financing the equipment you purchase from them or by leasing the equipment to you. However, be careful and remember that they are in the business of selling equipment when you analyze their plans and recommendations. On the other hand, many companies do have professionals that will give you good advice—and it's usually free. You may also want to hire a professional food facilities designer. Since the design and decor of the facilities—both the front of the house and the back of the house—will have a major impact on both the operating efficiencies and the ambiance the guest experiences, be certain the improvements to the facilities are well thought out.

Start Your Hiring Process

If you have some hiring to do, start now. Sixty days is usually long enough to allow for hiring the right person.

Use Job Descriptions

A job description is a short description of the job you wish to fill, focused on the skills, education and experience needed. A basic example is provided in Appendix A on p. 145.

Job descriptions are extremely valuable personnel tools. Writing a job description makes you pay attention to the job (Is it needed at all? What are the characteristics of a good applicant?) and avoid the pitfalls of discrimination legalities. Yes, you can be selective: You don't have to hire anyone you don't feel is both willing and able to do the job. No, you can't discriminate: Qualifications for the job must be applied in a fair, even-handed manner. Discrimination problems arise when different sets of standards are applied on the basis of race, gender, age, or other criteria.

Job descriptions also help you determine wage ranges, help you recruit from a pool of possible employees, and help you communicate with your employees once you've hired them. A job description doesn't have to tie your hands ("It's not in my job description" doesn't have a role in small business), but it does help make clear what a job involves, what its responsibilities and duties are.

Choose from More Than Three Applicants

Three is an arbitrary number, but if you have fewer than three qualified applicants for a job, you run a very high risk of making a poor hiring decision. Want ads, state and private employment agencies, vocational schools, colleges, word of mouth, and time provide enough candidates to help make good hiring decisions.

Schedule Interviews

Since you have to juggle a lot of balls at this time, scheduling becomes a problem. Don't depend on help appearing off the street. Set interview schedules and stick to them. Hiring is the biggest problem area for many business owners. A mistake is very costly (in terms of time and money), but it's not something that many people have had experience at. Interviews are even worse: it's easy to jump on the first good applicant. Don't! Try to find a hiring or personnel seminar or workshop and take it. And, most importantly, remember to check your applicants' references.

Our restaurateurs provided the following information to help you determine the qualifications you should look for when hiring waitstaff.

When hiring servers, how important are each of the following characteristics?

	"1"	"2"	"3"	"4"	"5"	Avg.
Attitude and personality	0.0%	0.0%	2.4%	25.0%	72.6%	4.7
Appearance	0.0%	2.4%	26.2%	47.6%	23.8%	3.9
References	9.5%	21.4%	45.2%	19.0%	4.8%	2.9
Previous restaurant experience	14.3%	25.0%	38.1%	17.9%	4.8%	2.7
Wage or salary demands	21.4%	32.1%	32.1%	11.9%	2.4%	2.4

"1" = Not Important
"2" = Slightly Important
"3" = Important
"4" = Very Important
"5" = Extremely Important

Their responses send a pretty strong message. To be certain, we asked them the following question, "Of the five attributes listed above, which is the most important to consider when hiring servers?" They responded:

92.9%	Attitude/Personality
3.6%	Experience
3.6%	Appearance
0.0%	References
0.0%	Cost

WOW! There's no doubt about what's important! What they are really saying is that it's easy to train a pleasant, friendly person to be a good server but it's nearly impossible to train a grump to be friendly and pleasant. Enough said.

Refine Your Mission Statement

Go back to your mission statement. Does it still fit? Feel right? Express what your restaurant should become? You will have increasing reasons to have a clear mission statement in the next few weeks. Set some time aside to review it with your advisors. It's time well spent, even if your decision is to stick with the statement you already have.

You can use your mission statement as a guide to making decisions. If a proposed action doesn't further the accomplishment of the mission, question whether or not that action should be performed. Usually it shouldn't be.

Chapter Seven Action Plan

A. Concept Development (Type of Restaurant, Theme, Decor, Type of Service, etc.)

Action/Strategy	Target Date	Person Responsible	Results/ Comments
1. Finalize your ideas about type of restaurant, theme, decor, type of service, etc.			
2. Bounce these ideas off your advisory board (there's still time to change or refine them).			
3. Bounce these ideas off potential customers (there's still time to change or refine them).			
4. Contact printers about signage, stationery, and promotional materials.			
Add your own actions/strategies here.			

Action Plan, continued

B. Financial Issues (Pro Forma Income Statements, Cash Flow Statements, Balance Sheets, etc.)

Action/Strategy	Target Date	Person Responsible	Results/ Comments
1. Finalize your operating statement pro formas.			
2. Review it with your accountant.			
3. Finalize your cash flow pro forma.			
4. Review it with your accountant.			
5. Finalize your opening balance sheet.			
6. Review it with your accountant.			
Add your own actions/strategies here.			

Action Plan, continued

C. Operational Issues (Menu, Kitchen Design, Work Flow, Patron Flow, etc.)

Action/Strategy	Target Date	Person Responsible	Results/ Comments
1. Contact food and beverage vendors.			
2. File the necessary applications with vendors to establish credit.			
3. Begin to write your operations manual.			
4. Begin to write your employee handbook.			
5. Finalize your job descriptions.			
6. Place ads for hiring employees.			
7. Do preliminary screening of employees.			
8. Make sure remodeling and construction is progressing on schedule.			
9. Contact garbage removal services, gas and electric companies, telephone companies, and other utilities to make arrangements for their services.			
Add your own actions/strategies here.			

Action Plan, continued

D. Legal Issues (Legal Entity, Permits and Licenses, State and Federal Income and Personal Taxes, etc.)

Action/Strategy	Target Date	Person Responsible	Results/ Comments
1. Make sure you have applied for all required insurance coverage.			
2. Talk with you insurance agent about other coverage that may be desirable—even if not legally required.			
3. Check on status of liquor license.			
4. Check on status of health department permit.			
5. Meet with lawyer to review legal documents needed for your financing.			
Add your own actions/strategies here.			

Action Plan, continued

E. Personal Issues

Action/Strategy	Target Date	Person Responsible	Results/ Comments
1. Continue to update your general management skills.			
2. Continue to update your restaurant management skills.			
3. Discuss upcoming event with family.			
Add your own actions/strategies here.			

EIGHT

One Month Before Start-Up

IT TAKES AT LEAST A MONTH TO GET THE FINAL DETAILS thoroughly nailed down. Something will crop up unexpectedly; deliveries won't be made; leasehold improvements will take longer than planned; some legal snafu will pop up. Count on it.

How can you ensure that your business opening will be smooth?

The checklist approach is a start: Make a long list of what has to be done. Then work backwards to see when you should start doing each item. Allow extra time since schedules always slip. Your aim is to have a hassle-free opening. In business, as in any enterprise, well-begun is half-finished. Get off to the best start you can.

Fine Tune Your Cash Flow Budget

You will find that your budget needs a certain amount of tinkering on a steady basis, especially during the start-up months when experience begins to correct assumptions. Don't allow yourself to be paralyzed by aiming for perfection in your budgeting. Budgeting is a difficult art and science to master. You'll improve with time.

Check your sales forecast *again*. Most disbursements are predictable (within limits). The biggest variable to worry about is cash from operations. You can be more definite about cash from new loans or capital, and at this stage, cash from sale of fixed assets isn't likely. A common pattern for many start-up restaurants is a flurry of activity (due to start-up publicity and natural local curiosity—the honeymoon effect) followed by a slump that may last anywhere from two to six months as a steady repeat customer base develops.

As a general rule, the conservative approach to cash flow is best. Expect revenue to develop slowly. Expect expenditures to grow faster than you plan.

The cushion of working capital you build into your financing should see you through this period.

Set Up Variance Reports

Variance reports (see the sample on p. 196 in Worksheets at the back of the book) help you keep track of actual against budgeted performance on a monthly basis. Your accountant or other financial advisors will help you set this up for your business. If there is a sizable variation in any budgeted item, look into it. It may turn up to be a problem or an opportunity, and in either event, the sooner you are aware of what goes on, the better. As an example, if anticipated utility costs are much below what you expected, it could mean that the bill wasn't paid, or that the weather was unusually warm or cool for that time of year or that you over-budgeted. The point is that if you are aware of such deviations, you can make informed decisions and profit from these decisions.

The variance report also forces you to refer to your budget at least once a month. A surprising number of business owners don't use a budget (or don't have one), and, as a result, run out of cash. Don't be one of them.

You may wish to keep track of some variables such as sales, payroll cost, food cost, and cash position on a weekly or even daily basis. Mapping this information (using a graph with dollars on the vertical line, dates on the horizontal line) can be extremely informative over a period of time. (A computer makes this easy to do.) The cumulative impact of this kind of information is hard to beat.

You may want to follow some non-financial variables that will affect your business. Daily number of covers and average check are two that definitely should be tracked. There may be others.

The aim of these reports is not to drown you in paperwork (many of these reports take only a few minutes to prepare), but to make managing your new enterprise easier. In a going business, established routines and experience substitute for these reports and are not usually adequate substitutes at that. As the new restaurant on the block, if you do more things right than your competitors do, you'll get off to a fast start.

Prepare for Your Grand Opening

Plan ahead and be prepared. Whatever can go wrong, will.

Whatever type of restaurant you are planning to open, an opening ceremony of some kind is in order. You can get local press coverage for free; you gain an immediate presence in the community; and you get an invaluable chance to control the first impression your business makes.

You don't have to invest in marching bands and fancy balloons. A grand opening can be anything from mailed announcements to a circus, depending on what image you are trying to present.

Since this will be your first opportunity to publicize your start-up, make the best of it. Use your advisors. Ask your ad agency or marketing consultant to help you think it through. You only have one shot at this, so don't waste it.

Rehearse

A grand opening is a first cousin to a theatrical performance. You have to make sure that the premises are clean, kitchen equipment installed and operating, and personnel trained for the event. If you are still hiring the day you open the doors for business, make sure the new workers understand they will be making first impressions that affect the future of your business and their jobs.

- Make sure all food and beverage items are ordered—and on hand by opening day.

- Finalize arrangements with utility companies and vendors.

- Order flowers or other decorations a week early.

- Schedule grand opening hours. People need to know when to come and when to leave.

- Have collateral advertising material ready (brochures, business cards, take-out menus, or other handout material with the restaurant's name, address, phone number, and logo on it). Make sure your printer is aware of your deadline. You might want to set it two weeks before opening date. If the job needs to be changed or redone, you'll still be on schedule.

- Invite the local press 30 days ahead of time, with a follow-up invitation a week before the event. Make sure they receive whatever press release your advertising or marketing advisors recommend.

- Local politicians love to be photographed helping new businesses get started. Invite them.

- Follow up. For instance, a guest book for people to sign and leave their addresses in can become the basis for a mailing list. A "three-month (or one-year)-after-opening" story may interest your local paper.

Your grand opening is a marketing opportunity. Seize it.

Soft Opening

Many restaurants hold what is called a "soft opening." That is, they actually serve customers for several days to a week before their advertised opening date. Customers are friends and relatives that the owner invites or potential regular customers who just happen to wander in. The soft opening give the staff an opportunity to work the bugs out in both preparation and service. Thus, when the grand opening occurs, everyone knows their jobs and can give the paying customers a wonderful first experience—remember, you only have one chance to make a first impression! Of course the soft opening will involve expenses—labor, food, utilities, etc.—but they're well worth it to make sure everything and everyone is working smoothly.

We know of one restaurant that decided to open its doors—without advertising—a week before the grand opening and to serve everyone who came a free meal in exchange for their feedback about the experience. Word quickly spread and by the second day people were lined up in the street and waiting two hours to get in. The restaurant ran out of food and couldn't possibly serve everyone. The restaurant got lots of free publicity in the local papers (that's the good news) but managed to get quite a few potential customers upset by not being able to serve them. We don't recommend quite so large a soft opening.

Do Your Final Professional Check

The less you have to worry about the better. About two weeks before opening, ask your professional advisors (lawyer, accountant, insurance agent, and SCORE, SBDC, SBA, or other consultants) for a final check.

- Ask your lawyer to check that all licenses have been acquired, codes satisfied, and other legal odds and ends have been attended to. One reason you need a lawyer with a small business practice is that these checks are routine, and he or she can perform them quickly, thoroughly, and inexpensively. While you could save a few dollars by doing them yourself, the risk isn't worth the savings.

- Have your accountant or other financial advisor review your bookkeeping set up, basic information system, and compliance with tax requirements. There may be last-minute changes or adjustments that will serve you well. If not, you know that things are in order and ready to go.

- Are all legally required insurance coverages in place, and the optional coverages you and your insurance advisor have decided upon bound? Careful attention to these small details now can save you big grief later. Arrange for an insurance review on at least an annual basis; this is the first.

- Ask your marketing and other consultants, formal or informal, to review your opening strategy, operating plans, and financing with you. At this late date you may not be able to effect any big changes before opening, but if you have been careful, this session will provide a lot of reassurance. It can also plug some small gaps. Anything you can do to improve the odds of success is worth doing.

Hire Your Staff

Hiring is a tricky business. You don't want to meet a payroll if it isn't necessary, yet you may have to staff up and train your employees before start up. Last month you began the recruiting and interviewing process, and may have made some hiring decisions. This month, the problem is hiring people (including negotiating wages), getting those persons up to speed, and preparing them for the opening. One of the advantages of a soft opening is that it provides the opportunity to train staff.

Compensation

Broadly interpreted, compensation includes salary or wages, working conditions, opportunities for advancement, fringe benefits, training, and even a social component. As a small business owner you have some latitude in what you offer to make your business attractive to employees, but you can't compete directly with a Fortune 500 company in terms of pay or benefits.

You can compete effectively in terms of offering an interesting, varied, concerned, and convenient working environment. A few guidelines are:

- *Use pay ranges.* As a rule, you get what you pay for. Local pay ranges can be established by questioning other business owners, keeping track of want ads, checking with state employment agencies, and even by asking private employment agencies. Sometimes large businesses in your area will divulge wage range information. A pay range for each job should set a bottom and top figure. Within that range, wages will vary according to the experience of the applicant, your needs, availability of labor, and a number of other factors. Offering more than other businesses won't necessarily get you the best applicants and will set a precedent that's hard to maintain. It will get you the hungriest applicants, who will stick with you only until a better offer comes along (and it will).

- *Use training.* If you used job descriptions in the hiring process, spotting areas where additional training is needed will be simplified. Training, especially wait person training, has such a fast, high payoff that not providing it is a foolish economy. More important, offering training shows the employees that you are interested in their development. Good employees appreciate the chance to improve their skills. You benefit from better employees; they benefit from a chance to get ahead. Gaining a reputation as a good trainer is a powerful long-term employment strategy.

- *Use employee benefits.* You can offer flexible hours, shared jobs, compensation time, or other benefits that don't cost much but are important to your employees. The range of possible fringe benefits goes all the way from vacation and holiday pay to education and training to insurance

Besides servers, we also asked about hiring the people who will be preparing the food.

When hiring chefs or cooks, how important are each of the following characteristics?

	"1"	"2"	"3"	"4"	"5"	Avg.
Attitude and Demeanor	0.0%	2.4%	10.8%	32.5%	54.2%	4.4
Experience	6.0%	9.6%	34.9%	31.3%	18.1%	3.5
Managerial Ability	4.8%	9.6%	34.9%	33.7%	16.9%	3.5
Creativity	7.2%	10.8%	38.6%	32.5%	10.8%	3.3
Personal References	9.6%	16.9%	41.0%	25.3%	7.2%	3.0
Formal Training	19.3%	27.7%	31.3%	13.3%	8.4%	2.6

"1" = Not Important
"2" = Slightly Important
"3" = Important
"4" = Very Important
"5" = Extremely Important

As with the servers, the message was that attitude and demeanor were the most important. Again, to be certain, we asked them the following question, "Of the six attributes listed above, which is the most important to consider when hiring a chef or cook?" They responded:

61.0%	Attitude and Demeanor
19.5%	Experience
8.5%	Managerial Ability
6.1%	Formal Training
4.9%	Creativity
0.0%	Personal References

Apparently many of our respondents had either heard about the "temperamental chef" and either didn't want to experience such a person or had experienced one and didn't want to experience another!

and pension programs to child care and sick leave. Small businesses can be more flexible than big companies—an advantage for you.

Keep in mind that benefits once granted are hard to pull back. What do other local employers offer? What are the costs? Can you make the benefits contingent on performance?

Know the Importance of Customer Service

A familiar business saying is: "Rule One is that the customer is always right. Rule Two is that if the customer is wrong, see Rule One." Customers are your business. They are your most valuable asset. And they are easily lost.

All employees should be trained in customer service from Day One. Before start up, this is even more important. You want to establish a reputation for putting the customer first if your business is to prosper.

- *Train all your employees to be courteous.* The role of common courtesy is often overlooked. Some restaurants such as Durgin Park in Boston have thrived with surly waitresses. It's a deliberate part of their ambiance. Most restaurants couldn't get away with it. Don't even try!

- *Make sure everyone knows the word-of-mouth fallacy.* The customer who feels poorly treated complains to an average of 11 other people. However, customers who receive courteous treatment usually take it for granted. If you remember that the secret of successful marketing is minimizing the opportunities for customer dissatisfaction, courtesy training is an important marketing tactic.

- *"Coddle the customer"* because the customer makes your business. The customer pays the bills. The customer is boss. No customer, no business. And it costs roughly five times as much to acquire a new customer as to keep an old one. This is why L.L. Bean cheerfully refunds money or replaces merchandise to its customers without question. Stiff a customer and you run the risk of losing 11 others. Treat that customer right, and you retain a friendly ambassador.

- *Remember your hiring criteria.* Go back and review the hiring criteria in Chapter Seven.

Make Sure Everything Works

Before opening, run through as many procedures as you can. Is everything in place, plugged in, ready to go? It is easier to correct minor glitches before you open than later. This is another argument for having a soft opening.

Include Security Procedures

The Russian proverb "trust, but verify" applies to business as well as to international relations.

- Who opens and closes the restaurant?

- Set up procedures for making sure the coffee pot and all the other equipment is turned off, the alarms turned on, the doors locked and so forth.

- Arrange for periodic security checks.

- Ask your accountant to review cash handling and other sensitive business procedures.

Implement Marketing, Promotions, and Opening Plans

Congratulations! You are now a restaurateur!

Chapter Eight Action Plan

A. Concept Development (Type of Restaurant, Theme, Decor, Type of Service, etc.)

Action/Strategy	Target Date	Person Responsible	Results/ Comments
1. Implement promotional plans.			
2. Be certain all interior and exterior decor has been completed.			
Add your own actions/strategies here.			

Action Plan, continued

B. Financial Issues (Pro Forma Income Statements, Cash Flow Statements, Balance Sheets, etc.)

Action/Strategy	Target Date	Person Responsible	Results/ Comments
1. Review final financial projections with your accountant, banker, and advisory board.			
2. Set up a variance reporting system.			
3. Set up a management information system to provide you with the necessary data after opening.			
Add your own actions/strategies here.			

Action Plan, continued

C. Operational Issues (Menu, Kitchen Design, Work Flow, Patron Flow, etc.)

Action/Strategy	Target Date	Person Responsible	Results/ Comments
1. Be certain all renovations and remodeling has been completed.			
2. Prepare for the grand opening (or soft opening and then grand opening).			
3. Hire all staff.			
4. Train all staff.			
5. Make certain all equipment works.			
6. Finalize all arrangements with utility companies.			
7. Finalize all arrangements with vendors.			
8. Order menus, promotional materials, and other printed materials.			
9. Order initial food, beverage, and supplies inventories.			
10. Go through several dress rehearsals.			
Add your own actions/strategies here.			

Action Plan, continued

D. Legal Issues (Legal Entity, Permits and Licenses, State and Federal Income and Personal Taxes, etc.)

Action/Strategy	Target Date	Person Responsible	Results/ Comments
1. Be certain all necessary permits and licenses are obtained and properly displayed.			
2. Be certain all necessary tax identification numbers have been obtained.			
3. Be certain all necessary insurance policies are established.			
4. Review everything with your accountant, banker, and lawyer.			
Add your own actions/strategies here.			

Action Plan, continued

E. Personal Issues

Action/Strategy	Target Date	Person Responsible	Results/ Comments
1. Take the time to discuss pertinent issues with your family.			
2. Get some rest!			
Add your own actions/strategies here.			

NINE

Start-Up and After

DON'T CHANGE YOUR PLANS WITHOUT STRONG REASONS.

In the first few months your restaurant is in operation, you may be busier than you ever have been or will be again. The key to getting through these months successfully: Maintain your focus. You spent months deciding what your business is, who your markets are, and what (and why) they will buy from you. You decided what promotions made sense, what kind of image to project, and what to do if things didn't go exactly as planned.

Under the press of daily business, with experience correcting your forecasts (often in a negative way), it becomes very tempting to try to do a little more, change your menu, go after a different market, buy market share, or any of thousands of possible responses to outside forces. Be stalwart. Stick to your plan for three months. That gives you enough time (in most cases) to get over the initial excitement of running your own business, meet the payroll and other fixed expenses several times, and have a better grip on what your business patterns actually will be.

Sales may be higher than anticipated initially, followed by a substantially lower sales pattern than hoped for. This is a common pattern and doesn't mean that your plans were off the mark. Initial sales often come from the newness factor, and after the novelty for your customers wears off, sales will slowly build in a more normal pattern. Assuming that you did your home-work in the pre-start-up period, these swings will even out.

Some ways to keep your enthusiasm high include scheduling your time effectively (that is, doing the right things at the right times), updating your product/benefit list from your customers' viewpoint, and paying extra attention to communications with your markets. Expect to make mis-takes—you're human. But plan to learn from your mistakes (and from your successes). You will learn more about the restaurant in the first three to six months than you will in the next five years. That's exhilarating.

Budget Your Time

Within the first month of operation you'll find certain habits and patterns emerging: You go to work, open the door, and how do you spend your time? Time is a finite—and precious—resource, and your best investment is budgeting your own time to make sure you don't leave any major aspect of your business undernourished. In successful businesses every important management area is given adequate attention. Unsuccessful businesses are lopsided. We all prefer to spend time doing things we enjoy doing, and try to avoid (if possible) those tasks we dislike. This poses a simple choice: either budget your time to avoid those gaps, or don't manage your time and wake up in a sweat at 3:00 A.M. wondering if you remembered to fill in that tax form or make that loan payment.

When budgeting your time, keep these points in mind:

- The tasks of management are: to plan, coordinate, direct, control, monitor, evaluate, correct, review, and innovate. These areas require attention on a regular basis.

- Set aside time for your family and for yourself to avoid burnout. The temptation to spend all your time at work is beguiling, but the costs in personal terms are excessive. Build in some down time for yourself as well. Getting away from the hurly burly of business pays off in having better judgment and making better decisions. This is particularly important in the restaurant business, where you will be up early to buy produce and up late to shut the door after your last guest leaves.

- Set aside time for learning more about your business (information pays). You can never know too much about your business, the restaurant industry, and general management and economic issues.

- Set aside time to get to know your customers better. Talk with them. Ask them questions; listen to their answers. There's a good reason you have two ears and one tongue. Listen twice as much as you talk, and you'll become wise. Make sure to get as many of their names and addresses as possible, as well as information about their interests and preferences for marketing purposes.

- Set aside time to research your competition. The more you know about your competition, both direct and indirect, the better. Religiously maintain those competitor files. Shop your competition. Speak with their customers and suppliers. They act as a mirror for your own business's improvement.

Continuously Update Your Menu and Service Level

This is where your interests and those of your customers intersect. If you remain attuned to their wants and preferences and shape your restaurant to their needs, you win. But use fine tuning, not radical surgery. Remember all that research you have done? If you try to force what you happen to have to sell on a public that doesn't want to buy, you're in deep trouble.

Listen

To customers

To your family and friends

To your employees

To vendors

To competitors

To advisors

And listen to yourself. People like to give advice. Your role as business owner is to listen, *evaluate* what you hear, and act accordingly based upon your judgment and experience. This is not a recommendation that you weigh every bit of input equally. You learn from others, selectively, by applying the intelligence and experience that urged you to go into business on your own in the first place.

Check Cash Flow Budget Against Actual Performance

The budget imposes a discipline that is especially important when you are in the early stages of operation and times are tight. "If in doubt, do without" isn't a bad motto, especially when you're backed up by a cash flow budget that shows what you can and cannot afford to do.

Ask your accountant to set up a deviation analysis program to follow. In deviation analysis, you compare, line item by line item, actual as compared to projected performance. Your cash flow budget is a projected set of figures; actual performance will differ, but usually not drastically. By faithfully comparing these two sets of figures monthly (or more often), you accomplish two important objectives: You become aware of exactly what is going on financially in your restaurant, and you learn what those changing numbers reveal about operations. Financial statements properly used have great power.

Update Your Plans as Needed

Losing focus is the biggest danger small business owners run.

Plan your restaurant carefully, follow your plan, and make adjustments only if necessary. The main thrust of your plan, as embodied in your mission statement and long-term objectives, should not change. The urge to change it to take advantage of an opportunity or add some cash to the till is hard to resist.

Before making any radical changes in what your business does, check with your advisory board, discuss the proposed actions with your SCORE or SBDC or similar counselors, and make sure your banker is alerted.

Maintain Good Communications with Your Banker and Vendors

The basic rule for dealing with your banker, vendors, and investors is simply the Golden Rule: Do unto others as you would have others do unto you. It's good business. Treat them the way you like to be treated: honestly, fairly, and consistently.

Work with Your Banker

Your bank will be one important source of money for your restaurant. Accordingly, you have to choose and nurture a banker. Your relationship with your banker has to be based on factual information as well as on some intangibles, but above all keep in mind that bankers do not like surprises. Keep your banker informed about bad news as well as good, and about any major changes in the way you do business. The results will be worth the effort.

Bankers have to be satisfied on two key questions:

1. Does this loan make sense for the business?

2. How will the loan be repaid? If things don't work out, what's the secondary repayment source?

Some common misconceptions about banks are that they only will lend you money when you don't need it, that they are insensitive to start ups (and restaurants in general), and that they want to own your house and other possessions. Unprepared applicants seldom get the financing they think they deserve; people expect the bank to whittle down their loan requests, so they ask for far too much in the first place, which destroys their credibility right off the bat.

Matching the Term of Your Loan to Your Financing

Your banker will match the financing with the reason for the financing. A bankerly rule of thumb is *never borrow short-term to meet a long-term obligation, and never borrow long-term to cover a short-term obligation.*

- Short-term loans are used for short-term needs: **inventory loans**, with repayment to come from selling the inventory, are usually 30 to 90 days. Short-term cash flow gaps are often covered by **short-term notes secured by receivables**. (Chronic cash flow shortages reflect undercapitalization or poor cash management. Both are serious problems that your banker will want you to solve as soon as possible.)

- Your banker will suggest a **line of credit** to simplify paperwork if you will have occasion to borrow short-term frequently. A line of credit works much the same as a credit card, except that you have to pay it off in full at least once a year.

- **Equipment loans** are repaid from operating profits over a period not to exceed the life of the equipment. These are usually set up as **term loans**, with fixed payments made on a regular working basis, over one to seven years. **Working capital loans** are treated the same way.

- **Mortgages** are **long-term loans** used to purchase real estate and may extend up to 15 years. In some cases long-term loans are used to purchase major equipment.

Ask your banker for help, explaining that your plans and your cash flow indicate your need for a loan. Put the banker on your team. Your banker is experienced in financial areas that you are not (he or she will see 200 or more business loan applications each year) and has a vested interest in seeing you succeed. Bankers always want their small business customers to become bigger businesses.

Banks are not venture capitalists or charitable organizations. They make their profit by renting out their depositors' money. They can't make a profit if they don't get the money back, so they are conservative, avoid risky ventures and long shots. Their fiduciary relationship to their depositors forbids them from such investments. And legally, they cannot lend into negative net worth businesses.

Bankers have been trained in observing the Five Cs of Credit for many years. Become aware of their concerns and you will have a better probability of securing the kind of financing that will help your business grow (and grow profitably).

The Five Cs of Credit

1. **Character.** Loans to small businesses are not commercial loans in the sense that they are made to individuals, not to businesses. Many bankers claim that in fact they never lend to small businesses, but rather are investing in the owner on the basis of knowing that person's character. Ultimately, the owner will be responsible for repayment of loans. You will find that you have to sign personally as a guarantor of any bank loan your business secures. The kind of person you are has a lot to do with the kind of reception you will get at the local bank. If you have a reputation for being honest, straightforward, and responsible, you will probably get your loan application approved.

2. **Credit.** Your credit history is a key piece of the puzzle for your banker. How have you handled credit in the past? If you have paid your debts more or less on time, don't have a history of bankruptcy or creditor lawsuits, and have proven that you can use credit effectively, your banker will be somewhat eased. A good credit record seldom causes the banker to make a loan, but a bad record will cause him or her to deny credit.

3. **Capacity.** How much debt can you take on safely, and how much can your business bear? Remember that small business loans tend to be made on the basis of the individual's ability to support that debt rather than on the strength of the business's cash flow. A careful cash flow projection will shift much of the burden to the business, but your banker will still look to you as the ultimate source of repayment. Your banker will ask for a personal financial statement as well as your business's balance sheet and cash flow in order to figure out how much you can afford to borrow. They are the experts, so listen to them. They don't want to burden you with too much debt because they want you to succeed.

4. **Capital.** You have to have at least as much at risk as the bank or other investors. This doesn't mean that your borrowing capacity is limited to what you can put in personally, but it does mean that you have to have some of your own cash (plus, in some cases, the cash investment from other investors) in the deal. The "creative financing, 100 percent or 110 percent leveraged deal" is not for business owners who plan to succeed. Your banker may ask you to secure more capital before a loan can be granted. Permanent capital (including subordinated debt) provides a cushion for the business and gives your banker a sense of security about lending you money.

5. **Collateral.** Your banker doesn't want to own your business or house or securities. He or she is in the banking business. Collateral is taken for two reasons: security (reduction of perceived risk to the bank) and commitment. Collateral represents a source of repayment in the worst case scenario (which reduces the risk of extending the credit in the first place). By putting up collateral, you show that you are at least as committed to the success of the venture as you expect the bank to be.

Work with Your Vendors

Your vendors will be your largest source of credit. Most restaurants purchase inventory and services on credit and come to rely on their vendors to "bank" them during periods of tight or negative cash flow.

You will find that you can't get much trade credit at first, but by punctilious payment of bills in small amounts, you will be able to enjoy customary trade credit over time. Remember that your vendors are in business to make money and will respond the same way you do to evasive payment habits.

Make a vendor list and avoid becoming dependent on one or two vendors. Comparison shopping is as good for your restaurant as for your personal purchases. And it helps when times get tight.

If you hit a hard cash flow problem, level with your vendors. Ask for their tolerance and you will almost surely receive it; they are aware that it costs about five times as much to get a new customer as to retain an old one, and they want you to make a go of your business. Small, consistent progress payments are a lot better than saying, "The check is in the mail," "I sent you the wrong check," or "The bookkeeper is on vacation and took the checkbook."

In more normal times, look closely at the terms of the sale. If your vendors offer 2%/10, net 30, and you can afford to take the discount, you'll earn about 36% per year. Ask your banker. *Careful purchasing habits often provide all of the restaurant's profits.* Of course you have to look at your cash flow, inventory levels, and so on before making purchase and payment decisions.

Working with Investors

Investors, like bankers, don't like surprises. If you have a drastic change in plans, or if your projections get thrown off by unexpected competition, a hurricane, or other major disaster, let them know. Fast. They want you to make a go of your business and, if kept informed, will do their best to make your business succeed.

If something good happens, let them know. Fast. Don't save the good news for a time when you have to

A final—but important—note from our survey. We asked our restaurateurs, "Based upon your experience, if you were starting all over again, which one planning area would you concentrate on the most?" We were surprised by their answers which follow:

32.1%	Operations (standard operating procedures, training, and control systems).
27.2%	Financial Issues (type, amount, and sources of financing).
24.7%	Concept Development (planning and research).
16.0%	Marketing (understanding your customer and promoting your restaurant).

The attention to establishing operating systems is often overlooked in the planning stages—but shouldn't be. We have developed the Restaurant Facilities and Operational Review that is included as Appendix A to help you. Use it in the planning process to make sure you've addressed each of the items and use it after you open to be certain you are following good operating procedures.

say "Which do you want first, the good news or the bad?" They may be able to help you capitalize on the good news, and will remember it when you have bad.

Summary

Welcome to the club. Successful restaurants such as yours will be aren't the result of good fortune. As Arnold Palmer observed, "The more I practice, the luckier I get." Success (and luck) comes from hard work on the basics:

• Use information to balance your intuitions and hunches.

• Place your customers' interests and concerns above all else.

• Plan to meet those concerns profitably.

• Implement your plan.

• Thoughtfully adapt to change.

To succeed and thrive, your restaurant must grow in the direction and at the pace you feel is right for you and it. You've already taken the steps that assure maximum chances for success. Planning uses all of your skills, both right-brained (creative and intuitive) and left-brained (analytic and reasoning). Your creative side will be constantly challenged as your restaurant grows and economic and competitive climates change. The discipline imposed by your analytic side will channel that creativity and create the kind of business you deserve. Rely too heavily on either side and you'll act half-wittedly.

Have fun. One measure of restaurant success is the joy you bring to the job each day. Few activities are as exciting and challenging—or as much work— as making a restaurant prosper. The hard work you put in isn't drudgery. It's part of the pleasure of making your restaurant really hum.

And remember: you make your own luck. That is the best part of all. You (and you alone) control your future. Your income isn't dependent on a performance evaluation and salary schedule. Growth of your net worth isn't contingent on the vagaries of the stock market or a profit-sharing plan. You build your business, you reap the rewards.

Good luck. You'll make it work.

Restaurant Facilities and Operational Review

THE FOLLOWING RESTAURANT FACILITIES AND OPERATIONAL REVIEW contains over 700 items dealing with the facilities and operating policies and procedures for your restaurant.

Each question is designed for you to answer yes, no, or N/A (for not applicable). The correct answer to each question is yes—unless, of course, it is not applicable for your particular situation. If your answer is no, use the "Action(s) Needed" section to write down your action plan. It may also be helpful to write down a suggested date for completing the actions.

Use the review to help you plan your restaurant and to review the operations once you have opened. For example, the question, "Do emergency exit signs work?" should remind you that you need to plan for such signs during the planning and construction phases of your restaurant. The same question will serve to have you check for burnt-out bulbs in the emergency exit signs once you have opened and started operations.

The review is designed to make sure you have control of the restaurant's facilities and operation both during planning and once you are open. Use it often. Discuss your findings with your department heads and other key staff. Put together a plan for making the necessary corrections. And check to be certain that the corrections have been made in a timely manner.

The table of contents on the following page should help you find the appropriate section.

Restaurant Facilities and Operational Review

Table of Contents

Item	Yes	No	N/A	Action(s) Needed
Section I: Physical Facilities—Exterior				
1. Are there written opening and closing procedures?				
2. Have they been reviewed in the past year?				
3. Have the appropriate employees been instructed regarding opening and closing procedures?				
4. Is signage appropriate?				
5. Is signage visible and well lit?				
6. Is the building facade/exterior clean and freshly painted?				
7. Are building windows clean?				
8. Are entry doors clean?				
9. Is entry door signage clear?				
10. Is exterior lighting adequate?				
11. Are exterior lighting fixtures clean?				
12. Are driveway and sidewalks well-marked?				
13. Are driveway and sidewalks free of debris and stains?				
14. Are sidewalks in good repair?				
15. Are flower beds weeded?				
16. Are flower beds free of debris?				
17. Are shrubs and plantings healthy?				
18. Do trees need pruning?				
19. Are fences in good repair and freshly painted?				
20. Are all outside lights working?				
21. Are shutters in good repair and freshly painted?				
22. Are steps clearly marked and visible?				
23. Is outdoor furniture clean and in good repair?				
24. Are awnings clean and in good repair?				
25. Is the roof in good repair?				
26. Are gutters clean and in working order?				
27. Are sprinkler systems working?				
28. Are sprinkler systems set so they do not cover the sidewalk?				
29. Is the trash removal area screened from public view?				
30. Is the trash removal area clean?				
31. Is the delivery area clean?				
32. Are guest parking lots clean?				
33. Are parking spaces in guest parking lots well-marked and freshly painted?				
34. Are guest parking lots well lit?				
35. Are handicapped parking spaces well-marked?				
36. Are employee parking lots clean?				
37. Are parking spaces in employee parking lots well-marked and freshly painted?				
38. Are employee parking lots well lit?				
Section II: Physical Facilities—Interior—Front-of-the-House				
Lobby/Entry Area				
1. Are entry doors clean?				

Item	Yes	No	N/A	Action(s) Needed
2. Do entry doors close properly?				
3. Are windows clean?				
4. Is brass and other hardware clean and in good repair?				
5. Is the lobby appearance neat and orderly?				
6. Is lobby furniture in good repair?				
7. Are furniture cushions turned regularly?				
8. Are all lighting fixtures working?				
9. Are all light globes/shades of the same type?				
10. Is lobby art straight?				
11. Is lobby art glass clean?				
12. Are frames clean?				
13. Is there good lighting for viewing art?				
14. Are lobby plants and flowers healthy?				
15. Is lobby paint in good condition?				
16. Is lobby wallpaper in good repair?				
17. Are lobby moldings in good condition?				
18. Is lobby ceiling in good condition?				
19. Are lobby staircases in good repair?				
20. Is lobby carpet or tile in good repair?				
21. Is carpet free of spots, stains, and buckling?				
22. Are wall fixtures free of spots, smudges, and dust?				
23. Are door and window frames free of chips, scratches, cracks, dust, and spots?				
24. Are door and window tracks clean and operable?				
25. Are draperies properly hung?				
26. Are draperies clean?				
27. Are tables clean and polished?				
28. Are tables free of chips and scratches?				
29. Are telephones in working order?				
30. Are telephones clean?				
31. Are directions for use of telephones posted nearby?				
32. Are pads of paper and pens available adjacent to phones?				
33. Are telephone books adjacent to phones?				
34. Are telephone books in clean binders?				
35. Is signage accurate?				
36. Does signage provide necessary information (restrooms, coat room, telephones, exit, etc.)?				
37. Is signage well lit?				
38. Is signage dusted and polished?				
39. Is there adequate signage for special events?				
40. Do emergency exit signs work?				
41. Do fire-exit doors have crash bars?				
42. Is heating/AC equipment in good repair?				
43. Is the burglar alarm working?				
44. Is the coatroom well lit?				

Item	Yes	No	N/A	Action(s) Needed
45. Is the coatroom clean?				
46. Is the hostess/host stand well-lit?				
47. Is the hostess/host stand clean and free of chips, scratches, and smudges?				
48. Are fire extinguisher locations clearly marked?				
49. Are fire extinguishers properly charged?				
Public Restrooms				
1. Are the floors swept, clean, and mopped?				
2. Are the commodes/urinals/sinks clean with no leaks, drips, or stains?				
3. Are mirrors clean and free of cracks?				
4. Are vanity surfaces clean and free of cracks?				
5. Are appropriate restroom amenities available and adequately stocked?				
6. Are soap dispensers clean and not dripping?				
7. Are paper supplies adequate (towels, tissues, toilet tissues)?				
8. Are paper dispensers clean?				
9. Are trash receptacles emptied frequently to prevent overflowing?				
10. Are restrooms odor-free?				
11. Are walls and doors clean?				
12. Are doors properly hung?				
13. Is wall paint or paper in good repair?				
Bar/Lounge				
1. Is the overall appearance neat and orderly?				
2. Are entry doors clean?				
3. Do entry doors close properly?				
4. Are windows free of spots, streaks, and dirt?				
5. Is brass and other hardware clean and in good repair?				
6. Is the bar in good repair?				
7. Are bar finishes free of chips, wear, scratches, dust, and dirt build-up?				
8. Are back-bar mirrors and shelves clean and free of spots, streaks, and dirt?				
9. Are bar stools sturdy?				
10. Are bar stools free of dust and dirt build-up?				
11. Are tables sturdy?				
12. Are table finishes free of chips, wear, scratches, dust, and dirt build-up?				
13. Is the upholstery in booths free of spots, stains, and tears?				
14. Are booth frames free of dust and dirt build-up?				
15. Do bar stool styles match?				
16. Do chair styles match?				
17. Are drapes, shades, and blinds clean?				
18. Are sidestands free of chips, wear, scratches, dust, and dirt build-up?				
19. Are light fixtures free of spots, dust, and tarnish?				
20. Are all lighting fixtures working?				
21. Are all light globes/shades of the same type?				
22. Is wall paint clean and in good condition?				
23. Is wallpaper clean and in good condition?				
24. Are moldings clean and in good condition?				

Item	Yes	No	N/A	Action(s) Needed
25. Are ceilings clean and in good condition?				
26. Is carpet or tile in good condition?				
27. Is carpet free of spots, stains, or buckling?				
28. Are plants and flowers healthy?				
29. Are wall fixtures free of spots, smudges, and dust?				
30. Are door and window frames free of chips, scratches, cracks, and dust?				
31. Are door and window tracks clean and operable?				
32. Are draperies hung properly?				
33. Are draperies clean?				
34. Is signage accurate?				
35. Does signage provide necessary information (restrooms, telephones, exit, etc.)?				
36. Is signage well lit?				
37. Is signage dusted and polished?				
38. Do emergency exit signs work?				
39. Do fire-exit doors have crashbars?				
40. Is heating/AC equipment in good repair?				
41. Are fire extinguisher locations clearly marked?				
42. Are fire extinguishers properly charged?				
Dining Room				
1. Are entry doors clean?				
2. Do entry doors close properly?				
3. Are windows free of spots, streaks, and dirt?				
4. Is brass and other hardware clean and in good repair?				
5. Is the overall appearance neat and orderly?				
6. Is furniture in good repair?				
7. Are table finishes free of chips, wear, scratches, dust, and dirt build-up?				
8. Are tables sturdy?				
9. Is the upholstery in booths free of spots, stains, and tears?				
10. Are booth frames free of dust and dirt build-up?				
11. Do chair styles match?				
12. Are drapes, shades, and blinds clean?				
13. Are sidestands free of chips, wear, scratches, dust, and dirt build-up?				
14. Are light fixtures free of spots, dust, and tarnish?				
15. Are all lighting fixtures working?				
16. Are all light globes/shades of the same type?				
17. Is wall paint clean and in good condition?				
18. Is wallpaper clean and in good condition?				
19. Are moldings clean and in good condition?				
20. Are ceilings clean and in good condition?				
21. Is carpet or tile in good condition?				
22. Is carpet free of spots, stains, or buckling?				
23. Are plants and flowers healthy?				
24. Are wall fixtures free of spots, smudges, and dust?				
25. Are door and window frames free of chips, scratches, cracks, dust, and spots?				

Item	Yes	No	N/A	Action(s) Needed
26. Are door and window tracks clean and operable?				
27. Are draperies properly hung?				
28. Are draperies clean?				
29. Is signage accurate?				
30. Does signage provide necessary information (restrooms, telephones, exit, etc.)?				
31. Is signage well lit?				
32. Is signage dusted and polished?				
33. Do emergency exit signs work?				
34. Do fire-exit doors have crashbars?				
35. Is heating/AC equipment in good repair?				
36. Are fire extinguisher locations clearly marked?				
37. Are fire extinguishers properly charged?				
Section III: Physical Facilities—Interior—Back-of-the-House				
Hot Foods Area				
1. Is the overall appearance neat and orderly?				
2. Are entry doors clean?				
3. Do entry doors open and close properly?				
4. Is all equipment in good working order?				
5. Are all light fixtures working?				
6. Are light fixtures free of spots, dust, and dirt?				
7. Do all light fixtures have approved safety covers?				
8. Is wall paint clean and in good condition?				
9. Are ceilings clean and in good condition?				
10. Are floors swept and mopped?				
11. Are floor tiles free of cracks and loose grouting?				
12. Do emergency exit signs work?				
13. Do fire-exit doors have crashbars?				
14. Are floor drains free of debris and in working order?				
15. Are exhaust fans clean and free of dirt build-up?				
16. Are exhaust fans in proper working order?				
17. Are exhaust hoods clean and free of dirt build-up?				
18. Are exhaust hoods in proper working order?				
19. Is the fire suppression system clean and free of dirt build-up?				
20. Is the fire suppression system in proper working order?				
21. Has the fire suppression system been checked and certified within the appropriate time limit?				
22. Is the steam table in proper working order?				
23. Is the steam table clean and free of dirt build-up?				
24. Are all heat lamps in proper working order?				
25. Are all heat lamps clean and free of dirt build-up?				
26. Are all plate storage warmers in proper working order?				
27. Are all plate storage warmers clean and free of dirt build-up?				
28. Are all work tables sturdy?				
29. Are all work tables clean and free of dirt build-up?				

Item	Yes	No	N/A	Action(s) Needed
30. Is the grill in proper working order?				
31. Is the grill clean and free of dirt build-up?				
32. Are all ovens in proper working order?				
33. Are all ovens clean and free of dirt build-up?				
34. Are all steamers in proper working order?				
35. Are all steamers clean and free of dirt build-up?				
36. Are all fryers in proper working order?				
37. Are all fryers clean and free of dirt and grease build-up?				
38. Are all range burners in proper working order?				
39. Are all range burners clean and free of dirt build-up?				
40. Is the flat-top range in proper working order?				
41. Is the flat-top range clean and free of dirt build-up?				
42. Are all trunnion kettles in proper working order?				
43. Are all trunnion kettles clean and free of dirt build-up?				
44. Are dry storage areas clean and elevated off the floor?				
45. Are all refrigerators operating at the proper temperature?				
46. Are all refrigerators clean and free of dirt build-up?				
47. Are all freezers operating at the proper temperature?				
48. Are all freezers clean and free of dirt build-up?				
49. Have all freezers been defrosted recently?				
50. Is the hand washing area clean and free of dirt build-up?				
51. Does the handwashing area have the proper supplies?				
52. Is the first aid cabinet clearly marked?				
53. Is the first aid cabinet stocked with the proper supplies (bandages, tape, burn creme, etc)?				
54. Is shelving for storing chinaware and silverware clean and free of dirt build-up?				
55. Are fire extinguisher locations clearly marked?				
56. Are fire extinguishers properly charged?				
Cold Foods Area				
1. Is the overall appearance neat and orderly?				
2. Are entry doors clean?				
3. Do entry doors open and close properly?				
4. Is all equipment in good working order?				
5. Are all light fixtures working?				
6. Are light fixtures free of spots, dust, and dirt-build-up?				
7. Do all light fixtures have approved safety covers?				
8. Is wall paint clean and in good condition?				
9. Are ceilings clean and in good condition?				
10. Are floors swept and mopped?				
11. Are floor tiles free of cracks and loose grouting?				
12. Do emergency exit signs work?				
13. Do fire-exit doors have crashbars?				
14. Are floor drains clean and free of debris?				
15. Are exhaust fans clean and free of dirt build-up?				

Item	Yes	No	N/A	Action(s) Needed
16. Are exhaust fans in proper working order?				
17. Are all work tables sturdy?				
18. Are all work tables clean and free of dirt build-up?				
19. Are all ice baths in proper working order?				
20. Are all ice baths clean and free of dirt build-up?				
21. Are all dry storage areas clean and elevated off the floor?				
22. Are all refrigerators operating at the proper temperature?				
23. Are all refrigerators clean and free of dirt build-up?				
24. Are all freezers operating at the proper temperature?				
25. Are all freezers clean and free of dirt build-up?				
26. Have all freezers been defrosted recently?				
27. Is the hand washing area clean and free of dirt build-up?				
28. Does the hand washing area have the proper supplies?				
29. Is the first aid cabinet clearly marked?				
30. Is the first aid cabinet stocked with the proper supplies (bandages, tape, burn cream, etc.)?				
31. Are fire extinguisher locations clearly marked?				
32. Are fire extinguishers properly charged?				
Dish Machine and Pot Sink Area				
1. Is the overall appearance neat and orderly?				
2. Is all equipment in good working order?				
3. Are all light fixtures working?				
4. Are light fixtures free of spots, dust, and dirt?				
5. Do light fixtures have approved safety covers?				
6. Is wall paint clean and in good condition?				
7. Are ceilings clean and in good condition?				
8. Are floors swept and mopped?				
9. Are floor tiles free of cracks and loose grouting?				
10. Do emergency exit signs work?				
11. Do fire-exit doors have crashbars?				
12. Are floor drains free of debris and in working order?				
13. Are exhaust fans clean and free of dirt build-up?				
14. Are exhaust fans in proper working order?				
15. Are sinks clean and free of dirt build-up?				
16. Do sinks have signs listing proper water temperatures?				
17. Do sinks have warning signs posted explaining how to properly handle knives and hot pots and pans?				
18. Is the garbage disposal clean and free of dirt build-up?				
19. Is the garbage disposal in proper working order?				
20. Does the garbage disposal have operating instructions posted?				
21. Does the garbage disposal have warning signs posted?				
22. Does the garbage disposal have a well-marked emergency shut-off switch?				
23. Does the garbage disposal have a silver catcher/magnet installed?				
24. Is the soiled dish table sturdy?				

Item	Yes	No	N/A	Action(s) Needed
25. Is the soiled dish table clean and free of dirt build-up?				
26. Are dish racks in good repair?				
27. Are dish racks stored off the floor?				
28. Are glass racks in good repair?				
29. Are glass racks stored off the floor?				
30. Are silverware racks in good repair?				
31. Are silverware racks stored off the floor?				
32. Is the dish washing machine clean and free of dirt build-up?				
33. Is the dish washing machine in proper working order?				
34. Does the dish washing machine have operating instructions posted?				
35. Does the dish washing machine have warning signs posted?				
36. Are rubber floor mats provided at the dish machine?				
37. Does the dish washing machine have a well-marked emergency shut-off switch?				
38. Is the pot washing machine clean and free of dirt build-up?				
39. Is the pot washing machine in proper working order?				
40. Does the pot washing machine have operating instructions posted?				
41. Does the pot washing machine have warning signs posted?				
42. Are rubber floor mats provided at the pot machine?				
43. Does the pot washing machine have a well-marked emergency shut-off switch?				
44. Are chemicals and cleaning supplies properly stored and separated from food supplies?				
45. Are instructions posted for the proper handling of chemicals and cleaning supplies?				
46. Is the first aid cabinet clearly marked?				
47. Is the first aid cabinet stocked with the proper supplies (bandages, tape, burn creme, etc.)?				
48. Are fire extinguisher locations clearly marked?				
49. Are fire extinguishers properly charged?				
Dry Storage Area				
1. Is the overall appearance neat and orderly?				
2. Are entry doors clean?				
3. Do entry doors open and close properly?				
4. Are all light fixtures working?				
5. Are all light fixtures free of spots, dust, and dirt?				
6. Do all light fixtures have approved safety covers?				
7. Is wall paint clean and in good condition?				
8. Are ceilings clean and in good condition?				
9. Are floors swept and mopped?				
10. Are floor tiles free of cracks and loose grouting?				
11. Are floor drains clean and in working order?				
12. Is heating/air conditioning functioning properly?				
13. Is shelving sturdy?				
14. Is shelving clean and free of dirt build-up?				
15. Are all supplies stored on shelves rather than on the floor?				

Item	Yes	No	N/A	Action(s) Needed
16. Is there proper security for the area?				
Cold Storage—Walk-in and Reach-in Refrigerators				
1. Are exterior surfaces clean and free of built-up dirt?				
2. Are all interior surfaces clean and free of built-up dirt?				
3. Is the temperature proper?				
4. Are all light fixtures working?				
5. Do all light fixtures have approved safety covers?				
6. Is the compressor clean and free of dust and dirt build-up?				
7. Is there good air circulation around the compressor?				
8. Are all drains and drainage lines clear and working properly?				
9. Do all doors close properly?				
10. Are all door seals in good repair and functioning properly?				
11. Are all security devices working properly?				
Freezer Storage—Walk-in and Reach-in Freezers				
1. Are exterior surfaces clean and free of built-up dirt?				
2. Are all interior surfaces clean and free of built-up dirt?				
3. Is the temperature proper?				
4. Are all light fixtures working?				
5. Do all light fixtures have approved safety covers?				
6. Is the compressor clean and free of dust and dirt build-up?				
7. Is there good air circulation around the compressor?				
8. Are all drains and drainage lines clear and working properly?				
9. Do all doors close properly?				
10. Are all door seals in good repair and functioning properly?				
11. Are all security devices working properly?				
Section IV: Operating Policies and Procedures—Front-of-the-House				
Staffing, General				
1. Is department fully staffed?				
2. Are staff members dressed appropriately?				
3. If staff members are to wear uniforms, are the uniforms in good condition?				
4. Are name tags being worn if required?				
5. Does cross-training take place?				
6. Are statistics maintained on hours worked for productivity analysis?				
7. Are competitive salary and wage reviews conducted periodically?				
8. If so, are salaries and wages competitive for similar jobs in the area?				
9. Do the staff members have the necessary competencies to do their jobs?				
10. Are the department heads communicating with management?				
11. Are the department heads communicating with staff?				
12. Are the department heads communicating with guests?				
13. Is each department head knowledgeable about departmental procedures?				
14. Is each department head reviewed annually by the general manager?				
15. Is there a departmental organizational chart?				
16. Are there written job descriptions for each position?				

Item	Yes	No	N/A	Action(s) Needed
17. Are there regularly scheduled departmental meetings?				
18. Are departmental employees reviewed at least annually by the department head?				
19. Is there an orientation program for new employees?				
20. Are employee personnel files updated and complete?				
21. Are employees who are out on lost time workers' compensation claims followed up on and brought back to work in some capacity as soon as possible?				
22. Is there a written employee warning procedure?				
23. Is the written employee warning system adhered to?				
24. Is general manager approval required prior to all terminations?				
25. Is there a written sexual harassment policy?				
26. Is there a single, designated provider for workers' compensation injuries?				
27. Is the OSHA log for reporting injuries kept current?				
28. Have all items on the last health department review been addressed?				
29. Are all employee health department certificates up-to-date?				
30. Are file copies of health department certificates maintained?				
31. Are all employees required to wash their hands after using the restroom?				
Valet Parking				
1. Are there written opening and closing procedures?				
2. Have they been reviewed and revised in the past year?				
3. Are numbered receipts available for controlling guests' keys and cars?				
4. Are they used?				
5. Are guests' car keys stored in a locked cabinet?				
6. Is access to the key cabinet properly controlled?				
7. Are employees' drivers licenses checked periodically?				
8. Are copies of employees' drivers licenses kept on file?				
9. Is there a proper insurance policy in effect for damage or theft of guests' cars?				
Host/Hostess Station and Cashier				
1. Are there written opening and closing procedures?				
2. Have they been reviewed and revised in the past year?				
3. Are customers greeted promptly and courteously?				
4. Is there a reservations book?				
5. Are guests asked for their seating preference (time, number in party, smoking or no-smoking, etc.)?				
6. Is there a sign-in/sign-out procedure for cash draws?				
7. Is it adhered to?				
8. Is there a log-in procedure for the cash register?				
9. Are numbered guest checks used?				
10. Are guest checks properly distributed and signed for?				
11. Is there a policy concerning missing guest checks?				
12. Is it followed and adhered to?				
13. Are guest checks matched with kitchen and bar duplicates?				
14. Is there a closed-circuit camera on the cash drawer?				
15. Is there a lock box for cash drops?				
16. Are cash drops made periodically?				

Item	Yes	No	N/A	Action(s) Needed
Dining Room				
1. Are there written opening and closing procedures?				
2. Have they been reviewed and revised in the past year?				
3. Are linens color-matched and in good condition?				
4. Are linens pressed and napkins neatly folded?				
5. Is chinaware free of chips, scratches, spots, or fading?				
6. Do all chinaware pieces match?				
7. Is glassware free of spots, chips, or cracks?				
8. Does glassware match?				
9. Is flatware free of dents, spots, peels, and tarnish?				
10. Does flatware match?				
11. Are menus in good condition (not tattered, dirty, or worn)?				
12. Are wine lists available and in good condition?				
13. Are guests greeted quickly and properly?				
14. Are drink orders taken promptly?				
15. Is water poured promptly?				
16. Are menus offered and specials explained?				
17. Does the service staff upsell appetizers, wines, desserts, and high-profit items?				
18. Are there incentives for the service staff to upsell?				
19. Are there signature items for which the restaurant is well known?				
20. Are all holidays promoted to maximize guest reservations?				
21. Are themed special events planned during non-holiday seasons?				
22. Is there a formal method for obtaining feedback from the guests about the food, beverages, and service?				
23. Are there policies for handling certain problems such as excessive wait, wrong orders, and wrong preparation?				
24. Are tables cleared promptly after each course?				
25. Is the check presented in a timely fashion?				
26. Do bartenders and liquor servers receive proper training concerning not serving intoxicated people?				
27. Is liquor served only during the hours allowed by the liquor license?				
28. Are all liquor licenses, health permits, and other permits up-to-date?				
29. Are there procedures established for handling cash and credit cards?				
30. Are they adhered to?				
Bar/Lounge				
1. Are there written opening and closing procedures?				
2. Have they been reviewed and revised in the past year?				
3. Is glassware free of spots, chips, or cracks?				
4. Does glassware match?				
5. Are linens color-matched and in good condition?				
6. Are linens pressed and napkins neatly folded?				
7. Is chinaware free of chips, scratches, spots, or fading?				
8. Do all chinaware pieces match?				
9. Are menus in good condition (not tattered, dirty, or worn)?				

Item	Yes	No	N/A	Action(s) Needed
10. Are wine lists available and in good condition?				
11. Are guests greeted quickly and properly?				
12. Are drink orders taken promptly?				
13. Does the service staff upsell appetizers, wines, specials, and high-profit items?				
14. Are there incentives for the service staff to upsell?				
15. Are there signature items for which the bar is well known?				
16. Is there a formal method for obtaining feedback from the guests about the beverages and service?				
17. Are there policies for handling certain problems such as spilled drinks, wrong orders, and wrong preparation?				
18. Are tables cleared promptly and periodically?				
19. Are checks presented in a timely fashion?				
20. Do bartenders and liquor servers receive proper training concerning not serving intoxicated people?				
21. Is liquor served only during hours allowed by the liquor license?				
22. Are all liquor licenses, health permits, and other permits up-to-date?				
23. Are there procedures established for handling cash and credit cards?				
24. Are they adhered to?				
25. Are portion control policies and procedures established?				
26. Are they adhered to?				
27. Are policies concerning not serving minors adhered to rigidly?				
28. Are policies and procedures established for handling unruly patrons?				
29. Is a telephone readily available to the bartender?				
30. Are emergency numbers posted at the telephone?				
31. Is there a control system or exchange system for stocking liquor at the bar?				
32. Is the bulk liquor storage room always locked?				
33. Are liquor bottles at the bar locked in cabinets when the bar is not staffed?				
34. Are beer coolers kept at the proper temperature?				
35. Is beer stock rotated?				
36. Are draught beer lines and taps washed and flushed periodically?				
37. Is there a camera on the bar area?				
38. Is there a camera on the cash drawer?				
39. Are new beverage items costed out?				
40. Have all beverage items been costed out within the past year?				
41. Do standardized beverage recipes exist?				
42. Are they followed?				
43. Are pictures of correct glassware for drinks, wine, etc. posted?				
44. Are portion controls in effect?				
45. Is there a policy concerning "free" drinks?				
46. Is it adhered to?				
47. Are beer and liquor inventories taken at least monthly?				
48. Is a member of management present and involved in taking the beer and liquor inventory?				
49. Are prices marked on beer and liquor when received?				
50. Is there a policy about employees drinking alcoholic beverages when on duty?				

Item	Yes	No	N/A	Action(s) Needed
51. Is it adhered to?				
52. Is there a policy about employees drinking alcoholic beverages when off duty?				
53. Is it adhered to?				
Banquets and Catered Functions				
1. Are budgets prepared in advance for each banquet or catered function?				
2. Are they compared to actual costs after the event?				
3. Are guarantees required?				
4. Are they adhered to?				
5. Are printed promotional materials up-to-date?				
6. Are price lists up-to-date?				
7. Are policies for surcharges for exceeding booked hours explained in advance?				
Section V: Operating Policies and Procedures—Back-of-the-House				
Staffing, General				
1. Is the department fully staffed?				
2. Are staff members dressed appropriately?				
3. If staff members are to wear uniforms, are the uniforms in good condition?				
4. Are name tags being worn if required?				
5. Does cross-training take place?				
6. Are statistics maintained on hours worked for productivity analysis?				
7. Are competitive wage and salary reviews conducted periodically?				
8. If so, are salaries and wages competitive for similar jobs in the area?				
9. Do the staff members have the necessary competencies to do their jobs?				
10. Are department heads communicating to management?				
11. Are the department heads communicating with staff?				
12. Are the department heads communicating with guests?				
13. Are the department heads knowledgeable about departmental procedures?				
14. Are the department heads reviewed annually by the general manager?				
15. Is there a departmental organizational chart?				
16. Are there written job descriptions for each position?				
17. Are there regularly scheduled departmental meetings?				
18. Are departmental employees reviewed at least annually by the department head?				
19. Is there an orientation program for new employees?				
20. Are employee personnel files updated and complete?				
21. Are employees who are out on lost time workers' compensation claims followed up on and brought back to work in some capacity as soon as possible?				
22. Is there a written employee warning procedure?				
23. Is the written employee warning system adhered to?				
24. Is general manager approval required prior to all terminations?				
25. Is there a written sexual harassment policy?				
26. Is there a single, designated provider for workers' compensation injuries?				
27. Is the OSHA log for reporting injuries kept current?				
28. Have all items on the last health department review been addressed?				
29. Are all employee health department certificates up-to-date?				

Item	Yes	No	N/A	Action(s) Needed
30. Are copies of health department certificates maintained?				
31. Are all employees required to wash their hands after using the restroom?				
32. Are hair restraining devices used by all employees?				
33. Are rubber gloves available for pot washing and handling cleaning solutions and chemicals?				
Quality/Cost Controls				
1. Are sales tracked by items sold?				
2. Is the menu reviewed and changed periodically to reflect guest preferences?				
3. Is there a standard mark-up on menu items?				
4. Are all new menu items costed out?				
5. Has the entire menu been costed out within the past year?				
6. Do standardized food recipes exist?				
7. Are they followed?				
8. Are pictures of food items posted for both kitchen employees and waitstaff?				
9. Are portion controls in effect?				
10. Are they followed?				
11. Is the back door locked at appropriate times?				
12. Are all bulk storage areas locked?				
13. Are all coolers locked?				
14. Are all freezers locked?				
15. Are adequate key controls in place?				
16. Is there a standardized presentation for entrees and garnishes?				
17. Are there written opening and closing procedures?				
18. Have they been reviewed and revised in the past year?				
19. Are all food orders placed by waitstaff either in writing or by computer?				
Purchasing				
1. Do written raw food specifications by item or product type exist?				
2. Are they adhered to?				
3. Are bids received and bid sheets reviewed?				
4. Is an explanation required for not accepting a low bid?				
5. Do bids meet predetermined specifications?				
6. Do written policies exist regarding purchasing for employees?				
7. Are they adhered to?				
8. Are par stocks established for standard items?				
Receiving				
1. Are all items checked for quality?				
2. Are all items checked for quantity?				
3. Are all items checked for weight?				
4. Are all items checked for condition?				
5. Is a receiving stamp used?				
6. Are all invoices approved by management?				
7. Are invoice prices verified to bid prices?				
8. Are extensions checked?				
9. Is product priced and dated prior to storage?				

Item	Yes	No	N/A	Action(s) Needed
Storage and Inventory				
1. Are all products dated?				
2. Are all open containers covered?				
3. Are cooked foods stored over raw foods?				
4. Are all products stored off the floor?				
5. Are products issued on a FIFO basis?				
6. Are chemicals stored separately from food?				
7. Are chemicals clearly and properly labeled to meet OSHA requirements?				
8. Are food and beverage inventories taken monthly?				
9. Does an independent (non-food and beverage department employee) participate in the inventory process?				
10. Are inventory discrepancies followed-up on immediately?				
11. Are china, silver, and glassware inventories taken periodically?				
Section VI: Payroll and Personnel Policies and Procedures				
General				
1. Is there an employee handbook outlining personnel policies and procedures?				
2. Are employees required to sign that they have received the handbook?				
3. Are the signed forms kept on file?				
4. Are all records kept in a safe and secure area?				
5. Are W-2's sent to employees on a timely basis?				
6. Are all federal, and state payroll forms filed on time?				
7. Are tip records kept accurately?				
8. Do all salaried employees adhere to wage and hourly guidelines?				
9. Have all salaried employees been reviewed in the past year for compliance?				
Payroll Controls				
1. Are department heads preparing work schedules?				
2. Are there staffing guidelines for preparing work schedules?				
3. Are there weekly staffing forecasting meetings?				
4. Are schedules approved in advance?				
5. Is a variance analysis between actual and forecasted payroll prepared?				
6. Is overtime approved in advance?				
7. Are proper overtime records kept?				
8. Do time card hours agree with the payroll register?				
9. Is time card addition correct?				
10. Are time cards initialed by each employee's supervisor to indicate approval?				
11. Are any alterations initialed by both the employee and the supervisor?				
12. Do base wages, plus any declared tips, equal minimum wage?				
13. Is overtime correctly calculated for tipped employees by eliminating any tip credit for overtime hours worked?				
14. Are tipped employees declaring weekly tips?				
15. Is there a tip reporting register signed daily by employees?				
16. Is W-4 withholding periodically updated and verified against the payroll register?				
17. Do current wage rates (personnel file) agree with payroll register?				
18. Do salary increases have required written approvals?				

Item	Yes	No	N/A	Action(s) Needed
19. Is payroll verified at least once per year by having employees personally sign for and receive checks from someone not involved in the payroll process?				
Personnel				
1. Do personnel folders include completed applications?				
2. Do personnel folders include completed reference checks?				
3. Do personnel folders include W-4 forms?				
4. Do personnel folders include documentation for other deductions?				
5. Do personnel folders include salary and wage change history?				
6. Do personnel folders include up-to-date vacation status?				
7. Do personnel folders include up-to-date sick-leave status?				
8. Do personnel folders include written documentation declining health insurance?				
9. Do personnel folders include applicable health/work permits?				
10. Do personnel folders include applicable licenses?				
11. Do personnel folders include written documentation that employee handbook has been received?				
12. Is there a separate file for I-9 forms?				
13. Are I-9 forms filed for every employee?				
14. Is supporting information removed before filing I-9 forms?				
15. Are new employees reviewed for insurance status when eligible (with employee signature required if insurance declined)?				
16. Are there pre-established employee review dates?				
17. Is there documentation for both voluntary and involuntary employee terminations?				
18. Are exit interviews conducted?				
19. Are appropriate unemployment claims contested?				
Section VII: Accounting Policies and Procedures				
General				
1. Do financial statements adhere to the uniform system of accounts for restaurants?				
2. Is an outside audit performed annually?				
3. Are financial statements prepared monthly?				
4. Is there a due date for completion?				
5. Are due dates met?				
6. Are monthly financial statements reviewed by appropriate management personnel?				
7. Is there an annual operating budget?				
8. Is the operating budget broken down into monthly segments?				
9. Are department heads involved in preparing budgets for their departments?				
10. Are monthly actual operating results compared to budget?				
11. Is there an annual cash flow budget?				
12. Is the cash flow budget broken down into monthly segments?				
13. Are monthly actual operating results compared to the cash flow budget?				
14. Is a capital improvements budget prepared and reviewed on an annual basis?				
15. Do department heads review their monthly financial statements?				
16. If so, are they required to provide a critique of the results?				

Item	Yes	No	N/A	Action(s) Needed
17. Is the accounting system computerized?				
18. If so, are back-ups made daily?				
19. Is a back-up copy stored off-premises?				
20. Is property and liability insurance bid out occasionally?				
21. Are real estate taxes periodically reviewed for possible assessment protest?				
22. Has a physical inventory been conducted for personal property in the past year?				
23. Are personal property asset schedules prepared?				
24. Are personal property asset dispositions reported properly for personal property tax returns?				
25. Do departmental monthly files contain sufficient support and audit trails for journal entries?				
26. Have the balance sheet accounts been reconciled to the current printout?				
27. Is the storage of old files and records in an accessible area and neatly arranged?				
28. Are old files properly boxed and referenced as to contents and destruction dates?				
29. Are old files stored under lock and key?				
30. Are old files protected from the elements?				
31. Are there files for each bank account with copies of the most recent resolutions and signature cards?				
32. Is more than one signature required on checks?				
33. Are duties segregated and periodically rotated for proper control?				
34. Is there an accounting procedures manual?				
35. Are signature stamps, if used, properly controlled?				
36. Does the restaurant maintain proper schedules and files on insurance?				
37. Does the restaurant maintain proper schedules and files for licenses and permits?				
38. Is a tickler file maintained for critical license renewal dates?				
39. Are proper files maintained on long-term debts, notes, and equipment leases?				
40. Do service contracts include protection for workers' compensation and product liability where applicable?				
41. Are certificates of insurance for outside contractors on file?				
42. Do they name the restaurant as additional insured?				
43. Are all current contracts on file?				
44. Is a tickler file maintained for contracts to ensure review prior to expiration?				
45. Are service contracts modified to protect the restaurant from automatic renewal provisions?				
46. Are the function books for private functions checked on a monthly basis by accounting to ensure all functions have been accounted for and billed properly?				
47. Are vending revenues and commissions properly recorded and controlled?				
48. Are gift certificates and coupons properly recorded and controlled?				
49. Is there a written key control program?				
50. Is it adequate?				
51. Is it adhered to?				
52. Are charge slips controlled and missing charge slips properly followed-up on?				
53. Are cash register tapes reconciled daily against guest checks and ordering duplicates?				

Item	Yes	No	N/A	Action(s) Needed
54. Is a purchase order system being used?				
55. If so, is it adequate and being enforced?				
56. Is there a written policy for purchasing?				
57. Are purchases coded in accordance with the chart of accounts?				
58. Are daily receiving reports used?				
59. Are invoices forwarded to accounts payable on a daily basis?				
60. Are all invoices received and booked in the appropriate month?				
61. Is sales tax being reported for employee meals?				
62. Are taxable purchases from out-of-state vendors properly reported?				
63. Are sales taxes being paid in a timely manner?				
64. Is there a system in place to track 1099 filing obligations?				
65. Are all 1099s sent on a timely basis?				
66. Does accounts payable audit invoices for accuracy and receipt of delivery before payment?				
67. Are invoices verified to the purchase orders for quantity and prices?				
68. Are bills paid from invoices and not from statements?				
69. Are the supporting documents canceled, attached to, and filed with the voucher copy?				
70. Are discounts being taken?				
71. Is a check request form used for disbursements which have no support (e.g., travel advances)?				
72. Are advance deposits properly recorded and supported?				
73. Do employee advances conform to policy?				
74. Are accounts being written off after all reasonable methods of collection have been exhausted?				
75. Are they being turned over to a professional collection agency if they warrant it?				
76. Is the bad debt write-off schedule properly maintained?				
77. Are credit procedures followed for outside and catering functions?				
78. Are all adjustments to charges approved by a supervisor?				
79. Are the names of persons and purpose of entertainment written on the guest check?				
80. Is there supervisor approval and reasons written on all comped guest checks?				
81. Is an aged listing of accounts receivable prepared monthly and reconciled?				
82. Are receivable files adequate and under secure control at all times?				
83. Are checks received by mail handled by someone other than the accounts receivable clerk?				
84. Is there a log for checks received in the mail?				
85. Is there independent verifying and initialing of the receipted bank deposit slip?				
86. Are lags in deposit times (other than armored car or bank holiday lag) being investigated or explained?				
87. Are bank accounts reconciled to the general ledger on a monthly basis?				

Item	Yes	No	N/A	Action(s) Needed
Section VIII: Risk Management				
General				
1. Is risk management a topic at every weekly department head meeting?				
2. Are all fire exits clearly marked?				
3. Are emergency power services tested weekly?				
4. Are safety procedures included in new staff orientation?				
5. Are any employees trained in CPR?				
6. Is there emergency resuscitation, first aid, and Heimlich maneuver training?				
7. Is there an employee safety committee?				
8. Does the committee conduct inspections at least every two months?				
9. Are safety committee recommendations implemented and documented?				
10. Has the insurance carrier been asked, within the past year, to make recommendations to limit liability?				
11. Have those recommendations been implemented?				
12. Are authorized automobile drivers listed on the insurance policy?				
13. Are all drivers checked for valid driver's license?				
14. Are stairwells free of obstructions?				
15. Is roof access properly marked?				
16. Is fire equipment clearly marked?				
17. Are fire extinguishers and systems tags current?				
18. Are current inspection reports on file?				
Emergency Procedures				
Are emergency and evacuation procedures written for each of the following potential situations?				
1. Fires?				
2. Bomb threats?				
3. Interruptions of electrical service?				
4. Telephone system outages?				
5. Elevator stoppages?				
6. Accidents/illnesses?				
7. Deaths (guests or employees)?				
8. Earthquakes?				
9. Tornados?				
10. Hurricanes?				
11. Gas leaks/interruption of service?				
12. Loss of water?				
13. Floods?				
14. Riots, protests, other potential disruptions?				

Sample Partnership Agreement and Corporate Checklist

THESE FORMS HAVE BEEN MADE AVAILABLE TO Upstart Publishing Company, by General Business Services, Inc., of Rockville, Maryland. General Business Services, Inc. and Edwin K. Williams and Company, Inc. comprise the Professional Services division of The Dwyer Group located near Waco, Texas. Their tax department is located in Columbia, Maryland, under the leadership of Kelley Snyder, CPA. The two companies provide the small business community with pertinent business and tax counseling guidance along with related accounting and payroll services. They do this through their network of more than 500 franchises located in all 50 states.

We have modified the forms. To obtain originals, ask your local GBS representative for GBS form 89927: Partnership Agreement, or GBS form 89929: Corporate Checklist.

Sample Partnership Agreement

Agreement made _____, 19___, between
_____, City of
_____, County of _____, State
of _____, and _____ of
_____ (address),
City of _____, County of _____,
State of _____, hereinafter referred to as partners.

Item One: Name, Purpose and Domicile

The name of the partnership shall be _____.
The partnership shall be conducted for the purposes of _____
_____. The principal place of
business shall be at _____ unless relocated
by majority consent of the partners.

Item Two: Duration of Agreement

The term of this agreement shall be for _____ years, commencing
on _____, 19__, and terminating on _____, 19__,
unless sooner terminated by mutual consent of the parties or by operation
of the provisions of this agreement.

Item Three: Contribution

Each partner shall contribute _____ dollars ($_____) on
or before _____, 19__ to be used by the partnership to establish
its capital position. Any additional contribution required of partners shall
only be determined and established in accordance with Item Seventeen.

Item Four: Books and Records

Books of accounts shall be maintained by the partners, and proper entries
made therein of all sales, purchases, receipts, payments, transactions, and
property of the partnership, and the books of accounts and all records of
the partnership shall be retained at the principal place of business as
specified in Item One herein. Each partner shall have free access at all
times to all books and records maintained relative to the partnership
business.

Item Five: Division of Profits and Losses

Each partner shall be entitled to _____ percent (____%) of the net profits of the business and all losses occurring in the course of the business shall
be borne in the same proportion, unless the losses are occasioned by the

willful neglect or default, and not mere mistake or error, of any of the partners, in which case the loss so incurred shall be made good by the partner through whose neglect or default the losses shall arise. Distribution of profits shall be made on the _____ day of _____ each year.

Item Six: Performance

Each partner shall apply all of his or her experience, training, and ability in discharging his or her assigned functions in the partnership and in the performance of all work that may be necessary or advantageous to further business interests of the partnership.

Item Seven: Business Expenses

The rent of the buildings where the partnership business shall be carried on, and the cost of repairs and alterations, all rates, taxes, payments for insurance, and other expenses in respect to the buildings used by the partnership, and the wages for all persons employed by the partnership are all to become payable on the account of the partnership. All losses incurred shall be paid out of the capital of the partnership or the profits arising from the partnership business, or, if both shall be deficient, by the partners on a pro rata basis, in proportion to their original contributions.

Item Eight: Accounting

The fiscal year of the partnership shall be from _____ to _____ of each year. On the _____ day of _____, commencing in 19____, and on the _____ day of _____ in each succeeding year, a general accounting shall be made and taken by the partners of all sales, purchases, receipts, payments, and transactions of the partnership during the preceding fiscal year, and of all the capital property and current liabilities of the partnership. The general accounting shall be written in the partnership account books and signed in each book by each partner immediately after it is completed. After the signature of each partner is entered, each partner shall keep one of the books and shall be bound by every account, except that if any manifest error is found therein by any partner and shown to the other partners within _____ months after the error shall have been noted by all of them, the error shall be rectified.

Item Nine: Separate Debts

No partner shall enter into any bond or become surety, security, bail or co-signer for any person, partnership or corporation, or knowingly condone anything whereby the partnership property may be attached or be taken in execution, without the written consent of the other partners.

Each partner shall punctually pay his or her separate debts and indemnify the other partners and the capital and property of the partnership against his or her separate debts and all expenses relating thereto.

Item Ten: Authority

No partner shall buy goods or articles into any contract exceeding the value _____ dollars ($_____) without the prior consent in writing of the other partners; or the other partners shall have the option to take the goods or accept the contract on account of the partnership or let the goods remain the sole property of the partner who shall have obligated himself or herself.

Item Eleven: Employee Management

No partner shall hire or dismiss any person in the employment of the partnership without the consent of the other partners, except in cases of gross misconduct by the employee.

Item Twelve: Salary

No partner shall receive any salary from the partnership, and the only compensation to be paid shall be as provided in Items Five and Fourteen herein.

Item Thirteen: Death of a Partner

In the event of the death of one partner, the legal representative of the deceased partner shall remain as a partner in the firm, except that the exercising of the right on the part of the representative of the deceased partner shall not continue for a period in excess of _____ months, even though under the terms hereof a greater period of time is provided before the termination of this agreement. The original rights of the partners herein shall accrue to their heirs, executors, or assigns.

Item Fourteen: Advance Draws

Each partner shall be at liberty to draw out of the business in anticipation of the expected profits any sums that may be mutually agreed on, and the sums are to be drawn only after there has been entered in the books of the partnership the terms of agreement, giving the date, the amount to be drawn by the respective partners, the time at which the sums shall be drawn, and any other conditions or matters mutually agreed on. The signatures of each partner shall be affixed thereon. The total sum of the advance draw for each partner shall be deducted from the sum that partner is entitled to under the distribution of profits as provided for in Item Five of this agreement.

Item Fifteen: Retirement

In the event any partner shall desire to retire from the partnership, he or she shall give _____ months notice in writing to the other partners and the continuing partners shall pay to the retiring partner at the termination of the _____ months notice the value of the interest of the retiring partner in the partnership. The value shall be determined by a closing of the books and a rendition of the appropriate profit and loss, trial balance, and balance sheet statements. All disputes arising therefrom shall be determined as provided in Item Eighteen.

Item Sixteen: Rights of Continuing Partners

On the retirement of any partner, the continuing partners shall be at liberty, if they so desire, to retain all trade names designating the firm name used, and each of the partners shall sign and execute assignments, instruments, or papers that shall be reasonably required for effectuating an amicable retirement.

Item Seventeen: Additional Contributions

The partners shall not have to contribute any additional capital to the partnership to that required under Item Three herein, except as follows: (1) each partner shall be required to contribute a proportionate share in additional contributions if the fiscal year closes with an insufficiency in the capital account of profits of the partnership to meet current expenses, or (2) the capital account falls below _____ dollars ($_____) for a period of _____ months.

Item Eighteen: Arbitration

If any differences shall arise between or among partners as to their rights or liabilities under this agreement, or under any instrument made in furtherance of the partnership business, the difference shall be determined and the instrument shall be settled by _____, acting as arbitrator, and his or her decision shall be final as to the contents and interpretations of the instrument and as to the proper mode of carrying the provision into effect.

Item Nineteen: Release of Debts

No partner shall compound, release, or discharge any debt that shall be due or owing to the partnership, without receiving the full amount thereof, unless that partner obtains the prior written consent of the other partners to the discharge of the indebtedness.

Item Twenty: Additions, Alterations, or Modifications

Where it shall appear to the partners that this agreement, or any terms and conditions contained herein, are in any way ineffective or deficient, or not expressed as originally intended, and any alteration or addition shall be deemed necessary, the partners will enter into, execute, and perform all further deeds and instruments as their counsel shall advise. Any addition, alteration, or modification shall be in writing, and no oral agreement shall be effective.

In witness whereof, the parties have executed this agreement on _____ the day and year first above written.

Courtesy of General Business Forms, Inc.

Corporate Checklist

A. The formation of a corporation constitutes the formation of a separate legal entity under state law. It is essential that the services of a competent local attorney be obtained to help the client file the Articles of Incorporation and meet the terms of the state law.

B. Below is a sample election for the corporation to be treated as a Section 1244 small business corporation. This is included so that the client may have it available to discuss with his or her attorney.

C. Following is a list of steps that will be necessary for a new corporation. It should not be deemed to be all inclusive. It is not intended to be used as substitution to the client for a competent attorney.

1. Incorporators: Have a meeting of the incorporators and determine the following:

   a. The corporate name

   b. The classes and number of shares to authorize

   c. Business purpose for which the corporation is formed

   d. Initial capital needed

   e. The directors

   f. Location of business

   g. The corporate officers and their salaries

   h. Check on thin incorporation

2. Determine start-up date: If the corporation is to take over a going business, a start-up date should be set at some time in the future, so that all steps can be taken without unnecessary haste.

3. Research the corporate name: Check at once with the Secretary of State to see if the corporate name is available.

4. Notify the following:

   a. Insurance company—have policies changed? May also be necessary to increase coverage.

   b. Creditors—inform all creditors of former business.

   c. Customers—inform all customers of former business.

   d. State and local authorities—such as the state unemployment and disability department and county assessor.

5. Transfer assets and liabilities: If the corporation is to take over a going business, determine what assets and liabilities are to be turned over to the corporation, and what shares or notes are to be issued in exchange.

Determine whether it qualifies as a tax-free exchange under IRC Sec. 3.

6. Select banks: Select bank or banks and furnish resolution authorizing who is to sign checks and negotiate loans.

7. Obtain identification number: File application for an identification number, Federal Form SS-4.

8. File for worker's compensation coverage.

9. File for unemployment insurance coverage.

10. Obtain any special licenses: Check on transfer of new license such as health department, liquor authority, Federal Alcohol, Tobacco, and Firearms (ATF), local business, etc.

11. File final returns: If the new corporation is taking over a going business, file sales tax, FICA tax, unemployment tax, and worker's compensation final returns for the old business after the corporation takes over the operation of the new business.

12. Determine federal unemployment requirements: Determine if final Form 940, employer's annual federal unemployment tax return, is to be filed on old business.

13. Sales tax: Obtain a new sales tax vendor's license on the first day of business. Do not use any tax stamps purchased by the former business and do not use the plate from the former business.

14. Tax elections:
    a. Election under Sub-Chapter S: Determine if the corporation is going to elect to be taxed as a partnership under Sub-Chapter S. If so, prepare and file Form 2553, Election by Small Business Corporation, within 30 days after the first day of fiscal year of date new corporation commences to "do business."
    b. Section 1244 stock: If the corporation is eligible, issue stock in accordance with a written plan included in the minutes.
    c. Year ending: Determine the date the corporation's year will end.
    d. Accounting: Determine the method of accounting the corporation will use.

Resources for Restaurateurs

*National Restaurant Association. *Uniform System of Accounts for Restaurants*, sixth revised edition, 1990. This revised edition covers an introduction to accounting statements, examples of these statements based on the uniform system of accounts, simplified record keeping, restaurant controls, and a chart of accounts.

*National Restaurant Association and Deloitte & Touche. *Restaurant Industry Operations Report, 1991.* National Restaurant Association, 1991. This annual report summarizes financial and operating data provided by members of the National Restaurant Association. The report includes specific financial information on full-menu and limited-menu tableservice restaurants, operators with no table service (fast-food), and cafeterias. National Restaurant Association, 1200 17th St., N.W., Washington, DC 20036, (202) 331-5900.

Grace Shugart. *Food for Fifty*. Macmillan, 1989. Provides basic information, recipes, and guidelines for preparing food in quantity. Specifically, the book discusses: weights, measures, recipe adjustment, menu planning, and recipes for special meals. Photographs and drawings are included to illustrate preparation techniques.

Costas Katsigris. *Pouring for Profit: A Guide to Bar and Beverage Management.* Wiley, 1983. Details on how to manage a bar and beverage operation efficiently and profitably. Planning, equipping, staffing, purchasing, managing inventory, and marketing are all discussed, along with approaches to drink design and selection. More than 150 drawings and photographs illustrate techniques and equipment.

Cornell Quarterly. *The Essentials of Good Table Service.* Cornell Hotel and Restaurant Administration Quarterly, Ithaca, New York, 1988. This pamphlet covers the essentials of American, French and Russian table service from personal grooming to the details of serving crépes suzette at the tableside. Buffet and banquet service are also discussed, along with special sections on napkin folding and decorative ice carving.

The Educational Foundation of the National Restaurant Association. *Applied Food Service Sanitation*, 4th edition. Wiley & Sons, 1991. Teaches principles and practices to help reduce food borne diseases and improve quality. The four sections cover sanitation and health, the serving of sanitary food, sanitary and safe food environments, and managing a sanitary and safe food service. Full of pictures and illustrations.

Jack D. Ninemeier. *Management of Food and Beverage Operations*, 2nd edition. American Hotel and Motel Association, 1990. Presents practical ideas for both commercial and institutional food-service operations. Covers menu design, nutrition, marketing, equipment, computers, and overall food cost.

Paul J. McVety. *Fundamentals of Menu Planning.* Van Nostrand Reinhold, 1989. Provides basic information about foods, management, and financing for menu planning. Intended to assist food-service managers in developing new menus. The numerous tables, forms and sample menus help instruct the reader and aid the book's discussion of nutrition, costing, merchandising, menu analysis and equipment selection.

Regina S. Baraban. *Successful Restaurant Design.* Van Nostrand Reinhold, 1989. This guide fully discusses both kitchen and dining room designs. The designs discussed integrate functional with aesthetic concerns. Sections of the book address design analysis and psychology, the customer's and management's perspective, and specific problem solving. Features color and black-and-white photographs.

World Wide Web. The World Wide Web can provide tremendous volumes of information to help you put together your business plan. The best place to get started is through the National Restaurant Association's web site at http://www.restaurant.org or through *Nation's Restaurant News'* web site at http://www.nrn.com

Upstart Resources

Upstart Publishing Company: These publications on proven management techniques for small businesses are available from Upstart Publishing Company, 155 North Wacker Drive, Chicago, IL 60606-1719, (312) 836-4400.

Entrepreneurial

The Restaurant Planning Guide, 2nd edition, Peter Rainsford and David H. Bangs, Jr., 1996. This book takes the practical steps of the *Business Planning Guide* and combines it with the expertise of Peter Rainsford, a professor at the Cornell School of Hotel Administration and restaurateur. Topics include: establishing menu prices, staffing and scheduling, controlling costs, and niche marketing. 160 pp., $22.95

Launching New Ventures: An Entrepreneurial Approach, Kathleen Allen, 1995. Innovative entrepreneurship text that enables the students to plan and start a world-class venture. This guide takes the reader from the first basic steps of developing an idea to creating a detailed business and marketing plan. Instructor's manual available. 496 pp., $63.95

Strategic Planning for the New and Small Business, Fred L. Fry and Charles R. Stoner, 1995. This highly practical text guides the reader through the strategic planning process using case histories and examples of actual businesses. Unique in that it is a strategy book aimed specifically for small businesses. Instructor's manual available. 256 pp., $47.95

Financial Essentials for Small Business Success, Joseph Tabet and Jeffrey Slater, 1994. This text stresses importance of common sense in overcoming the problems of poor record keeping and planning. Step-by-step guidance results in students learning to interpret financial reports and building the necessary financial tools for a profitable small business. Instructor's manual available. 272 pp., $19.95

Business Plans

Business Planning Guide, 7th edition, David H. Bangs, Jr., 1995. Designed for both beginners and more experienced practitioners, this is a vital tool for putting together a complete and effective business plan and financing proposal. Contains three complete sample business plans. Available on CD-ROM. Instructor's manual available. 224 pp., $22.95. Also available as book and CD-ROM set, $39.95, or CD-ROM only, $19.95.

Anatomy of a Business Plan, 3rd edition, Linda Pinson and Jerry Jinnett, 1996. The step-by-step approach assumes no prior knowledge of a business plan. This basic presentation enables the entrepreneur to prepare a start-up plan for a new small business or plan new strategies for an existing business. Instructor's manual available. 272 pp., $19.95

Market Plans

Market Planning Guide, 4th edition, David H. Bangs, Jr., 1994. Practical text that shows readers how to create an effective marketing plan suited to the business' goals and resources. Features complete marketing plans for two actual businesses. Instructor's manual available. 256 pp., $19.95

Target Marketing, 3rd edition, Linda Pinson and Jerry Jinnett, 1996. Text is a comprehensive guide to developing a marketing plan for your business. Broken into a simple three-stage marketing process of research, reach and retain. Instructor's manual available. 176 pp., $22.95

Start-Ups

The Start-Up Guide, 2nd edition, David H. Bangs, Jr., 1994. Walks students through every phase of small business start-up. Text is based on a hypothetical one-year process. 160 pp., $19.95. Also available as book and CD-ROM set, $39.95, or CD-ROM only, $19.95.

Steps to Small Business Start-Up, 3rd edition, Linda Pinson and Jerry Jinnett, 1996. One step at a time, the student learns the mechanics of business start-ups and gets started on everything from record keeping, marketing and business planning. Contains forms, examples and worksheets. Instructor's manual available. 256 pp., $22.95

Finance

The Cash Flow Control Guide, 2nd edition, David H. Bangs, Jr., 1990. Step-by-step guide to learning a cash flow control process for the small business. It uses a real-life example of a company that demonstrates how cash flow planning can smooth out some of the small business's roughest spots. 88 pp., $14.95

Keeping the Books, 3rd edition, Linda Pinson and Jerry Jinnett, 1996. Hands-on introduction to small business bookkeeping, which may be used with those who have no financial or accounting background. It covers all the essentials and provides numerous sample forms and worksheets. Instructor's manual available. 224 pp., $22.95

International

Export Profits, Jack Wolf, 1992. Comprehensive guide that simplifies the complex subject of exporting. It assumes no prior knowledge of international trade and with the aid or resources, examples and sample documents covers all the aspects of exporting. 304 pp., $19.95

Case Books

Cases in Small Business Management, 3rd edition, John de Young, 1994. More than 50 intriguing and useful case studies focusing on typical problems faced by small business managers every day. Problem solving is encouraged through end-of-chapter questions that lead students through an analysis of possible solutions. Instructor's manual available. 288 pp., $39.95

Problems and Solutions in Small Business Management, Editors of *Forum*, 1994. A collection of case studies selected by the editors of the small business journal, *Forum*. A problem drawn from an actual business is presented and then followed by three possible solutions written by experts from a variety of areas within the field of small business management. 192 pp., $36.75

Periodicals

In Business. A bimonthly magazine for small businesses, especially those with fewer than 10 employees. The publisher is J.G. Press, PO Box 323, Emmaus, PA 18049.

Inc. One of the leading small business magazines. 38 Commercial Wharf, Boston, MA 02110, (617) 248-8000.

D & B Reports. Excellent case studies and updated financial information for small businesses. Dun and Bradstreet, 299 Park Ave., New York, NY 10171, (212) 593-6724.

Small Business Reports. A monthly magazine with how-to articles for the owners/founders of start-up and smaller businesses, plus information on the latest legal and other developments in the business arena. Published by the American Management Association, 135 West 50th St., New York, NY 10020, (800) 262-9699.

Small Business Forum: Journal of the Association of Small Business Development Centers. Case studies and analyses of small-business problems gleaned from a nationwide network of small-business development professionals. Includes book reviews. Reprints available. Issued three times a year, $25.00 per year. University of Wisconsin, SBDC, 432 North Wake St., Madison, WI 53706.

Software

NEBS Software. Some of the best software for small businesses is the One-Write Plus® accounting and payroll software from NEBS. One-Write Plus generates over 60 reports and financial statements, many of which may be customized by the user. For more information contact NEBS Software, Inc., 20 Industrial Park Drive, Nashua, NH 03062, or call (800) 882-5254.

The Business Planning Guide Computer Spreadsheet Templates, 1993. Disk contains templates of all the financial statements used in *The Business Planning Guide*, designed for use with Lotus 1-2-3™, version 2.0 or later. Available for IBM compatible PC and Macintosh in 5¼" or 3½" disk. Order from Upstart Publishing Company, 155 North Wacker Drive, Chicago, IL 60606-1719, or call (800) 235-8866.

Additional Resources

Small Business Development Centers (SBDCs). Call your state university or the Small Business Administration (SBA) to find the SBDC nearest you. Far and away the best free management program available, SBDCs provide expert assistance and training in every aspect of business management. Don't ignore this resource.

SCORE, or Service Corps of Retired Executives. Sponsored by the U.S. Small Business Administration, provides free counseling and also a series of workshops and seminars for small businesses. Of special interest: SCORE offers a Business Planning Workshop, which includes a 30-minute video produced specifically for SCORE by Upstart Publishing and funded by Paychex, Inc. There are over 500 SCORE chapters nationwide. For more information, contact the SBA office nearest you and ask about SCORE.

Small Business Administration (SBA). The SBA offers a number of management assistance programs. If you are assigned a capable Management

Assistance Officer, you have an excellent resource. The SBA is worth a visit, if only to leaf through their extensive literature.

Colleges and universities. Most have business courses. Some have SBDCs, others have more specialized programs. Some have small-business expertise—the University of New Hampshire, for example, has two schools that provide direct small-business management assistance.

Comprehensive Accounting Corporation, 2111 Comprehensive Drive, Aurora, IL 60507. CAC has over 425 franchised offices providing accounting, bookkeeping and management consulting services to small businesses. For information, call (800) 323-9009.

Center for Entrepreneurial Management, 29 Greene Street, New York, NY 10013. The oldest and largest nonprofit membership association for small-business owners in the world. They maintain an extensive list of books, videotapes, cassettes and other small-business management aids. Call (212) 925-7304 for information.

Libraries. Do not forget to take advantage of the information readily available at your local library.

Glossary

"Acid Test" Ratio: Cash, plus other assets which can be immediately converted to cash, should equal or exceed current liabilities. The formula used to determine the ratio is as follows:

Cash + Receivables (net) + Marketable Securities

= Current Liabilities

The "acid test" ratio is one of the most important credit barometers used by lending institutions, as it indicates the ability of a business enterprise to meet its current obligations.

Aging Receivables: A scheduling of accounts receivable according to the length of time they have been outstanding. This shows which accounts are not being paid in a timely manner and may reveal any difficulty in collecting long-overdue receivables. This may also be an important indicator of developing cash flow problems.

Amortization: To liquidate on an installment basis; the process of gradually paying off a liability over a period of time, i.e., a mortgage is amortized by periodically paying off part of the face amount of the mortgage.

Assets: The valuable resources, or properties and property rights owned by an individual or business enterprise.

Balance Sheet: An itemized statement that lists the total assets, liabilities, and net worth of a given business to reflect its financial condition at a given moment in time.

Beverage Cost or Beverage Cost Percentage: Refers to the cost of the ingredients in a beverage expressed as a percentage of the selling price.

Capital: Capital funds are those funds that are needed for the base of the business. Usually they are put into the business in a fairly permanent form such as in fixed assets, plant and equipment, or are used in other ways that are not recoverable in the short run unless the entire business is sold.

Capital Equipment: Equipment used to manufacture a product, provide a service, or to sell, store, and deliver merchandise. Such equipment will not be sold in the normal course of business, but will be used and worn out or be consumed over time as business is conducted.

Cash Flow: The actual movement of cash within a business: cash inflow minus cash outflow. A term used to designate the reported net income of a corporation plus amounts charged off for depreciation, depletion, amortization, and extraordinary charges to reserves, which are bookkeeping deductions and not actually paid out in cash. Used to offer a better indication of the ability of a firm to meet its own obligations and to pay dividends, rather than the conventional net income figure.

Cash Position: See Liquidity.

Collateral: An asset pledged to a lender in order to support the loan.

Covers: The number of meals served in a given period of time. A restaurant that serves 120 lunches would be described as serving 120 covers at lunch.

Current Assets: Cash or other items that will normally be turned into cash within one year, and assets that will be used up in the operations of a firm within one year.

Current Liabilities: Amounts owed that will ordinarily be paid by a firm within one year. Such items include accounts payable, wages payable, taxes payable, the current portion of a long-term debt, and interest and dividends payable.

Current Ratio: A ratio of a firm's current assets to its current liabilities. Because a current ratio includes the value of inventories that have not yet been sold, it does not offer the best evaluation of the firm's current status. The "acid test" ratio, covering the most liquid of current assets, produces a better evaluation.

Debt: Debt refers to borrowed funds, whether from your own coffers or from other individuals, banks or institutions. It is generally secured with a note, which in turn may be secured by a lien against property or other assets. Ordinarily, the note states repayment and interest provisions, which vary greatly in both amount and duration, depending upon the purpose, source and terms of the loan. Some debt is convertible, that is, it may be changed into direct ownership of a portion of a business under certain stated conditions.

Demographics: (1) The statistical study of human populations, especially with reference to size and density, distribution and vital statistics.

Demographics: (2) Relating to the dynamic balance of a population, especially with regard to density and capacity for expansion or decline.

Demographic Segmentation: A marketing analysis that targets groups of prospects by factors such as gender, age, marital status, income, occupation, family size, and education (from *Forecasting Sales and Planning Profits*, Kenneth E. Marino).

Distribution: The delivery or conveyance of a good or service to a market.

Distribution Channel: The chain of intermediaries linking the producer of a good to the consumer.

Equity: Equity is the owner's investment in the business. Unlike capital, equity is what remains after the liabilities of the company are subtracted from the assets—thus it may be greater than or less than the capital invested in the business. Equity investment carries with it a share of ownership and usually a share in profits, as well as some say in how the business is managed.

Food Cost or Food Cost Percentage: refers to the cost of the raw food ingredients of an item expressed as a percentage of the selling price.

Gross Profit: Net sales (sales minus returned merchandise, discounts, or other allowances) minus the cost of goods sold.

Guaranty: A pledge by a third party to repay a loan in the event that the borrower cannot.

Income Statement: A statement of income and expenses for a given period of time. Also called a Profit and Loss Statement or Operating Statement.

Inventory: The materials owned and held by a business firm, including new materials, intermediate products and parts, work-in-process and finished goods, intended either for internal consumption or for sale.

Liquidity: A term used to describe the solvency of a business, and which has special reference to the degree of readiness in which assets can be converted into cash without a loss. Also called Cash Position. If a firm's current assets cannot be converted into cash to meet current liabilities, the firm is said to be Illiquid.

Loan Agreement: A document that states what a business can or cannot do as long as it owes money to (usually) a bank. A loan agreement may place restrictions on the owner's salary, on dividends, on the amount of other debt, on working capital limits, on sales, or on the number of additional personnel.

Loans: Debt money for private business is usually in the form of bank loans, which, in a sense, are personal because a private business can be harder to evaluate in terms of creditworthiness and degree of risk. A secured loan is a loan that is backed up by a claim against some asset or assets of a business. An unsecured loan is backed by the faith the bank has in the borrower's ability to pay back the money.

Long-Term Liabilities: These are liabilities (expenses to the business) that will not mature within the next year.

Net Worth: The owner's equity in a given business represented by the excess of the total assets over the total amounts owed to outside creditors (total liabilities) at a given moment in time. Also, the net worth of an individual as determined by deducting the amount of all his or her personal liabilities from the total value of personal assets. Generally refers to tangible net worth, which does not include goodwill, etc.

Note: The basic business loan, a note represents a loan that will be repaid, or substantially reduced 30, 60, or 90 days later at a stated interest rate.

These are short-term, and unless they are made under a line of credit, a separate loan application is needed for each loan and each renewal.

Partnership: A legal relationship created by the voluntary association of two or more persons to carry on as co-owners of a business for profit; a type of business organization in which two or more persons agree on the amount of their contributions (capital and effort) and on the distribution of profits, if any.

Positioning: A marketing method based on determining what market niche your business should fill, and how it should promote its products or services in light of competitive and other forces.

Pro Forma: A projection or an estimate of what may result in the future from actions in the present. A *pro forma* financial statement is one that shows how the actual operations of a business will turn out if certain assumptions are realized.

Profit: The excess of the selling price over all costs and expenses incurred in making a sale. Also, the reward to the entrepreneur for the risks assumed by him or her in the establishment, operations, and management of a given enterprise or undertaking.

Sole Proprietorship or Proprietorship: A type of business organization in which one individual owns the business. Legally, the owner is the business and personal assets are typically exposed to liabilities of the business.

Sub-Chapter S Corporation or Tax Option Corporation: A corporation that has elected under Sub-Chapter S of the IRS Tax Code (by unanimous consent of its shareholders) not to pay any corporate tax on its income and, instead, to have the shareholders pay taxes on it, even though it is not distributed. Shareholders of a tax option corporation are also entitled to deduct, on their individual returns, their shares of any net operating loss sustained by the corporation, subject to limitations in the tax code. In many respects, Sub-Chapter S permits a corporation to behave for tax purposes as a proprietorship or partnership.

Takeover: The acquisition of one company by another company.

Target Market: The specific individuals, distinguished by socio-economic, demographic, and/or interest characteristics, who are the most likely potential customers for the goods and/or services of a business.

Term Loans: Either secured or unsecured, usually for periods of more than a year to as many as ten. Term loans are paid off like a mortgage: so many dollars per month for so many years. The most common uses of term loans are for equipment and other fixed assets, for working capital, and for real estate.

Turns: (or turnover) refers to the number of times every seat in the restaurant was used during a given meal period. A restaurant with 100 seats that served 120 lunches would be described as doing 1.2 turns for lunch.

Working Capital: The difference between current assets and current liabilities. Contrasted with capital, which is a permanent use of funds, working capital cycles through your business in a variety of forms: inventories, accounts and notes receivable, and cash and securities.

Worksheets

THESE BLANK WORKSHEETS and forms are for you to fill out and use.

Computation of Selling Price and Food Cost Percentage by Menu Item

Food Item	"Q" A	Other Food B	Total Raw Food Cost $ C	Suggested Selling Price at X% Food Cost D	Actual Selling Price E	Projected Food Cost % (C÷E)x100

A   Compute the raw food cost of "Q," or all the food items included in the price of the meal, except for the main item. Included in the "Q" should be salad, starch, bread and butter, garnishes, and anything else that is included with the price of the entree.

B   Compute the raw food cost of the entree.

C   Add columns A + B.

D   Divide column C by the desired food cost percentage. For example, if you desire a 35% food cost, divide by 0.35.

E   Adjust the actual selling price up or down depending upon other factors, such as perceived value, high labor cost for that item, competitive prices in the market, etc.

F   Compute the projected food cost percentage by dividing column C by column E and multiplying by 100 for a percentage.

Cash Flow Projection Form

	JAN	FEB	MAR	APR	MAY	JUN	JUL	AUG	SEPT	OCT	NOV	DEC	Totals
Cash Receipts													
Food Sales													
Beverage Sales													
Sales Receivables													
Other Income													
Total Cash Receipts													
Cash Disbursements													
Cost of Sales, Food													
Cost of Sales, Beverages													
Controllable Expenses													
Payroll													
Employee Benefits													
Direct Operating Exp.													
Advertising and Promotion													
Utilities													
Administrative and General													
Repairs and Maintenance													
Occupancy Costs													
Rent													
Property Taxes													
Other Taxes													
Property Insurance													
Interest													
Other Deductions													
Total Cash Disbursements:													

Cash Flow Projection Form, continued

	JAN	FEB	MAR	APR	MAY	JUN	JUL	AUG	SEPT	OCT	NOV	DEC	Totals
Cash Flow From Operations													
Cash Receipts													
Less: Cash Disbursements													
Net From Operations													
Cash on Hand													
Opening Balance													
Plus: New Loan (Debt)													
Plus: New Investment													
Plus: Sale of Fixed Assets													
Plus: Net From Operations													
Total Cash Available													
Less: Debt Reduction													
Less: New Fixed Assets													
Less: Dividends to Stockholders													
Less: Stock Redemption													
Less: Loans to Officers													
Total Cash Paid Out													
Cash Position—Ending Balance													

Sales and Expense Forecast

	Daily	x 6 =	Weekly	x 50 =	Annually
Number of Seats					
Number of Meals per Day (Covers)					
Average Check (Food)					
Average Check (Beverage)					
SALES					
Daily Food Sales					
(covers x $ /cover)					
Daily Beverage Sales					
(covers x $ /cover)					
Total Sales					
EXPENSES					
Cost of Sales					
Cost of Food Sold (36%)					
Cost of Beverages Sold (30%)					
Total Cost of Sales					
Gross Profit					
Other Income					
Total Income					
Controllable Expenses					
Payroll					
Employee Benefits					
Direct Operating Expenses					
Advertising and Promotion					
Utilities					
Administration and General					
Repairs and Maintenance					
Income Before Occupancy Costs					
Occupancy Costs					
Rent					
Property Taxes					
Other Taxes					
Property Insurance					
Total Occupancy Costs					
Income Before Int. and Deprec.					
Interest					
Depreciation					
Restaurant Profit					
Other Deductions					
Income Before Income Taxes					

Projected Profit and Loss

	10% Lower	Expected	10% Higher
SALES			
Food Sales			
Beverage Sales			
Total Sales			
EXPENSES			
Cost of Sales			
Cost of Food Sold (36%)			
Cost of Beverages Sold (30%)			
Total Cost of Sales			
Gross Profit			
Other Income			
Total Income			
Controllable Expenses			
Payroll			
Employee Benefits			
Direct Operating Expenses			
Advertising and Promotion			
Utilities			
Administration and General			
Repairs and Maintenance			
Income Before Occupancy Costs			
Occupancy Costs			
Rent			
Property Taxes			
Other Taxes			
Property Insurance			
Total Occupancy Costs			
Income Before Int. and Deprec.			
Interest			
Depreciation			
Restaurant Profit			
Other Deductions			
Income Before Income Taxes			

Projected Cash Flow

	Before Opening	Monthly Operations	Annual Operations
Sources of Cash			
Personal Savings			
Bank Loan			
Food Sales			
Beverage Sales			
Total Sources			
Uses of Cash			
Leasehold Improvements			
Tables, chairs, chinaware etc.			
Operating Expenses			
Cost of Food Sold (36%)			
Cost of Beverages Sold (30%)			
Payroll			
Employee Benefits			
Direct Operating Expenses			
Advertising and Promotion			
Utilities			
Administration and General			
Repairs and Maintenance			
Rent			
Property Insurance			
Interest			
Total Uses			
Cash Flow (Sources–Uses)			

Balance Sheet

Opening Day, _____

ASSETS

Current Assets

Cash $

Food Inventory

Beverage Inventory

Supplies Inventory

   Total Current Assets $

Fixed Assets

Leasehold Improvements $

Furniture, chinaware, etc.

Preopening expenses

Total Fixed Assets $

Total Assets $

LIABILITIES and NET WORTH

Current Liabilities

   Accounts Payable $

    Total Current Liabilities $

Long-Term Liabilities

   Bank Loan $

    Total Long-Term Liabilities $

   Total Liabilities $

Net Worth

   Investment $

   Retained Earnings

    Total Net Worth $

Total Liabilities and Net Worth $

Personal Data Sheet

Name _____

Address _____

Telephone number _____ Years there _____

Marital status _____ Name of spouse _____ Dependents _____

Education

	Name and address	Grades completed/ diplomas/degrees obtained
High School		
Other		

Military service _____ Years _____

Highest rank obtained _____

Relevant training or work experience _____

_____

Work Experience

Business and address	Job title and duties	Supervisor	Dates

Trade, professional or civic membership and activities _____

_____

Hobbies, interests, other relevant information _____

_____

Use another sheet if necessary.

Credit Inquiry

Name _____ Date of birth _____

Address _____

Telephone number _____ Years there _____

Former Address _____

_____ Years there _____

Marital Status _____ Name of Spouse _____ No. dependents _____

Employer _____ Years there _____

Address _____

Phone _____ Kind of business _____

Position _____ Net income $/ _____

Former employer and address _____ Years there _____

Spouse's employer and address _____

Net income $/ _____ Other income sources: $/month _____

Account	Bank	Acct. No.	Balance
Checking			
Savings			

Auto owned (year and make) _____ Purchased from _____ $ _____

Financed by _____ Balance owed $ _____ Monthly Payment _____

Rent or mortgage payment/mo. $ _____ Paid to _____

Real estate owned in name of _____ Purchase price _____ Mtge. bal. _____

Credit references and all debts owed—other than above
(Bank, loan or finance cost, credit unions, budget)

Name	Address	Orig. amt.	Bal.	Mo. payment

Life insurance amount _____ Company _____

If co-maker for others, state where and for whom _____

Nearest relative or friend not living with you/relationship _____

Address _____

Cost of Living Budget

(Based on average month—does not cover purchase of any new items except emergency replacements.)

Detailed Budget

Regular Monthly Payments

House payments
(principal, interest, taxes, insurance) or rent .... $ _____

Car payments (including insurance) .... $ _____

Appliance, TV payments.. $ _____

Home improvement loan payments .... $ _____

Personal loan, credit card payments.. $ _____

Health plan payments.. $ _____

Life insurance premiums .... $ _____

Other insurance premiums .... $ _____

Savings/investments.. $ _____

Total .... $ _____

Household Operating Expense

Telephone.. $ _____

Gas and electricity.. $ _____

Water.. $ _____

Other household expenses, repairs, maintenance .... $ _____

Total .... $ _____

Personal Expense

Clothing, cleaning, laundry .... $ _____

Prescription medications.. $ _____

Physicians, dentists .... $ _____

Education .... $ _____

Dues.. $ _____

Gifts and contributions.. $ _____

(Continued)

Cost of Living Budget, continued

Travel .... $ _____

Newspapers, magazines, books .... $ _____

Auto upkeep and gas .... $ _____

Spending money and allowances .... $ _____

Miscellaneous .... $ _____

Total .... $ _____

Food Expense

Food—at home .... $ _____

Food—away from home .... $ _____

Total .... $ _____

Tax Expense

Federal and state income taxes .... $ _____

Other taxes not included above .... $ _____

Total .... $ _____

Budget Summary

A. Income gross

    Monthly total .... $ _____

Less expense:

Regular monthly payments .... $ _____

Household operating expense .... $ _____

Personal expense .... $ _____

Food expense .... $ _____

Tax expense .... $ _____

Monthly total .... $ _____

B. Monthly total expenses .... $ _____

Savings (A − B) .... $ _____

Variance Report

From the Income Statement
For the Month of _____

	A Actual for Month	B Budget for Month	C Deviation % (B-A)	D Deviation (C/B x 100)
Sales				
Less Cost of Goods				
Gross Profit on Sales				
Operating Expenses				
Variable Expenses				
Sales Salaries (commissions)				
Advertising				
Miscellaneous Variable				
Total Variable Expenses				
Fixed Expenses				
Utilities				
Salaries				
Payroll Taxes and Benefits				
Office Supplies				
Insurance				
Maintenance and Cleaning				
Legal and Accounting				
Delivery				
Licenses				
Boxes, Paper, etc.				
Telephone				
Miscellaneous				
Depreciation				
Interest				
Total Fixed Expenses				
Total Operating Expenses				
Net Profit (Gross Profit on Sales Less Total Operating Expenses)				
Tax Expense				
Net Profit After Taxes				

Index